Building Bulletin 98:

Briefing Framework for Secondary School Projects

incorporating secondary school revisions to
BB82: Area Guidelines for Schools

The key purpose of this document is to set out simple, realistic, non-statutory area guidelines for secondary school buildings (Part C) and grounds (Part D) which supersede those in Building Bulletin 82: Area Guidelines for Schools, published in 1996, and any revisions.

Following draft revisions and the publication of the Exemplar Designs for Schools, the recommended gross area of secondary school buildings has been further increased to an average of 18% above the maximum in 1996. Funding from the Department for Education and Skills (DfES) in 2005-06 and beyond, for instance in the Building Schools for the Future programme, will allow all new buildings to be built to these standards.

Simple graphs and formulae can be used to check that the number, size and type of rooms in both new designs and existing buildings are at least that recommended for six categories of usable space. These have been calculated to address the requirements, common to every school, of pupils with special educational needs (SEN) and disabilities, the school workforce and community use out of school hours. Similar standards are set for various categories of site area.

Crucially, a further 'float' is also recommended to accommodate the individual priorities of each school: whether facilities for the specialism or limited 'extended school' provision. Every mainstream school is expected to need at least the total net area recommended, which includes the 'float'. Some schools may then have further supplementary area over and above this, for instance for specially resourced SEN provision.

However, getting the area right is only part of creating facilities which support the educational aims and vision of each school. Design quality and appropriate specifications are also crucial. Part A of this bulletin offers a framework for every secondary school to develop a strategic masterplan, incorporating any future building project, whether major new buildings or minor refurbishments. Part B identifies the key issues that should be addressed in the brief to ensure that the design is in line with the organisation and preferences of the school.

The Government's continuing commitment to education is reflected in the recent sharp increases in capital funding for schools. In the light of this investment, it is now all the more crucial to ensure that any building project is in line with a long-term masterplan for the whole site.

The guidance in this bulletin will assist school staff and governors, with the help of Local Education Authorities (LEAs), dioceses, and building professionals, to develop a masterplan and a brief to the necessary detail and ensure that the priorities of the school are clearly expressed and can be carried through the design.

contents

Introduction

A good brief is the foundation for the success of any building project. The objective of the ongoing brief-making process is to clarify the intentions of the client and inform the design team of the requirements for the project[1].

This document is designed to assist headteachers, governors and other stakeholders in the creation of a brief for any major project in a mainstream secondary school, with particular emphasis on the following issues:

- Part A: the **process** of creating a brief, and how the brief for any building project should fit within a strategic masterplan based on the school's longer term vision for the future;

- Part B: the key **design criteria** that should be included in the brief to ensure that facilities are appropriate and adaptable to suit the changing circumstances of the future;

- Part C: minimum **building area** requirements for each of the six categories of space within the usable or net area, and for the remaining area of the buildings;

- Part D: minimum **site area** requirements for the various categories of outdoor spaces needed within the playing field area or net site area.

Side notes on each page give references to further information and guidance, including Exemplar Designs[2] and Room Data Sheets[3].

Context

It is important that the brief for any building project is seen in the context of the overall strategic masterplan, to avoid work being done in the wrong place or in the wrong order. It is equally important that the masterplan is in line with the aims of the Local Education Authority's (LEA's) Children and Young People's Plan, operational asset management plan (AMP) and other strategies, for instance for accessibility[4], community and sport.

1 What is a Brief? The NBS (National Building Specification) Educator states that 'briefing is the process of identifying a client's need and finding an appropriate solution. A brief is a product of that process and is produced at key points in the project and formalizes decisions and instructions in a structured document. The briefing process is iterative and moves from the general to the particular.' See www.nbseducator.co.uk/briefs/homebriefs.shtm.

2. Exemplar designs have been developed by some leading architectural practices working to a DfES brief, to improve the design quality of school buildings. The designs, including five secondary schools, are intended to develop a shared vision of 'Schools for the Future' and create benchmarks for well designed schools.

3. Room Data Sheets were developed for the exemplar design brief to identify the key design criteria for each room. The examples on the web site are indicative only, but they highlight the headings that should be considered at the detailed stage of the brief. See www.teachernet.gov.uk/exemplars.

4. The Disability Discrimination Act 1995, as amended by the Special Educational Needs and Disability Act 2001, introduced Part IV 'Education' which requires LEAs to have an Accessibility Strategy for schools to increase access to information, the curriculum and the physical environment for disabled pupils, over a three year period to March 2006.
See www.teachernet.gov.uk/wholeschool/sen/schools/accessibility/.

Acknowledgments

The guidance in this publication has been written and researched by the following team of DfES School Building and Design Unit building professionals, under the leadership of Mukund Patel.

Editor:
Beech Williamson

With assistance from:

Tamasin Dale	school grounds and formulae
Alison Wadsworth	furniture layouts informing room areas
Gill Hawkins	SEN issues
Richard Daniels	environmental issues
Nick Mayer	analysis

The Department would like to thank the following people who helped to in the preparation of the final copy:

d-squared architects	original graphic format and photography
Learning Through Landscapes	input to text and photography as marked
School Works	input to text
Sport England	input to specifications and text
Jenny Coldrick, NPS architects	input to masterplan
Commission for Architecture and the Built Environment (CABE)	
The Charter School, Southwark and Blenheim High School, Epsom	

We would also like to thank the following members of the steering group that advised on the draft revision of Building Bulletin 82: Area Guidelines for Schools, on which this guidance is based:

Michael Moore	Derby LEA
Mark Dolling and Ted Pawley	Milton Keynes LEA
Graham Dalton	Cardiff LEA
Peter Robson	Dorset LEA
Pat Gibson	Canterbury C of E Diocese
Paul Briggs	Hexham & Newcastle R C Diocese
Michael Lloyd	NAHT
Gary Redhead	SEO
Andrew Price	Jarvis Construction
Shirley Turner	RIBA Schools Forum and EBDOG
Georgina Franks	RIBA Schools Forum
John Waldron	RIBA Schools Forum

Part A: The Briefing Process

The initial strategic brief for any project will need to be written by the client team. It can then be developed with the wider design team as building professionals become involved[1].

Client team

Depending on the size and type of project, the client team will include:

- those responsible for the provision of pupil places and the school estate, usually the Local Education Authority (LEA) or diocese;

- the fund holder(s), who needs to be sure that the brief is achievable within the budget and allows for future changes (for instance in staff and organisation) and for community use;

- senior school staff and governors, who will need to ensure the design is suitable for the individual needs of the school;

- other stakeholders, for example community groups who may wish to use the facilities or those that could provide further funding for multi-agency provision on the school site, such as health or social services.

The users of the project, including pupils, should also be represented when formulating the brief[2].

Outcome-based Approach

The best approach to brief writing is to define as clearly as possible the desired outcomes for the project, rather than attempting to specify design solutions to achieve the outcome. This will ensure the best value from the inventive design capability of the design team and constructor. In a PFI scheme, the brief in the form of an 'output specification' will also ensure that the risk of achieving the outcome is transferred to the provider[3].

1. A useful introduction to the roles of those involved in building projects is A Guide for School Governors: Developing School Buildings, published by the Royal Institute of British Architects (RIBA). Available, quoting ref: WS/GFG, from: RIBA Policy and International Relations, 66 Portland Place, London W1N 4AD, price £6.50.

2. School Works produces material to help set up participatory design projects in schools. Useful publications include Learning Buildings and the Toolkit. See **www.school-works.org.** Learning through Landscapes is a charitable trust which also puts the participation of pupils and staff at the heart of their advice and publications on the development of school grounds, to support the curriculum and other activities. See **www.ltl.org.uk.**

3. The Public Private Partnership Programme (4ps) publish guidance for PFI briefs, which can also be useful for non-PFI schemes. See **www.4ps.co.uk.**

5

Figure A.1: Option Appraisal in Context

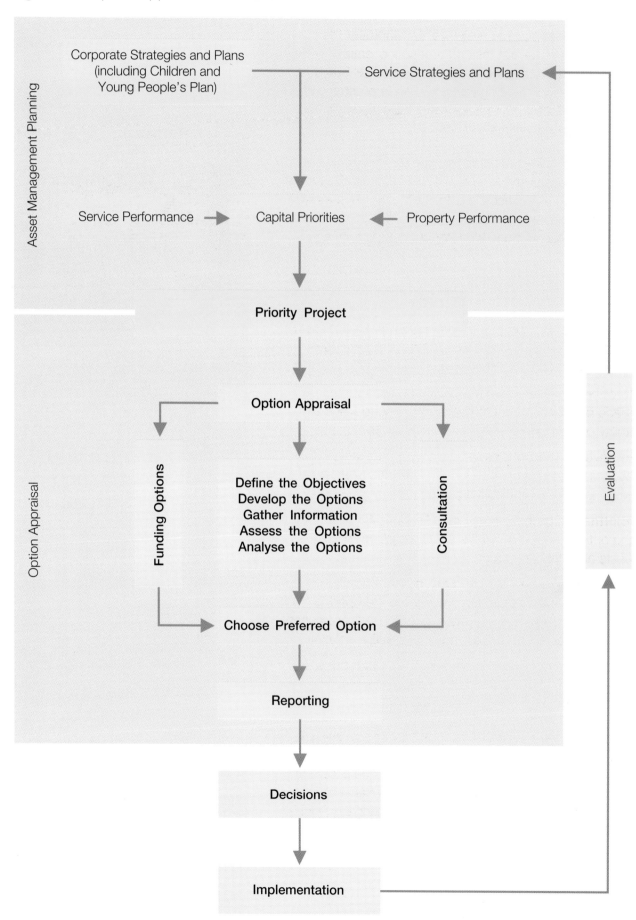

Preparing a Masterplan

A strategic masterplan, or Premises Development Plan (PDP), should be the first task for any school anticipating the need for improvements or alterations to their buildings or site. It will reflect the long term building implications of the school's education and community objectives, as set out in the School Development Plan.

To support the delivery of these objectives, all building projects – of whatever size or timescale – should then form part of this plan, like pieces in a jigsaw puzzle. This avoids early projects adversely affecting later ones, ensures best value and provides a framework for short-term funding opportunities.

Finding the Right Solution

The masterplan or PDP can be developed in the same way as any building project, following the steps of an Option Appraisal (as in figure A.1 opposite)[1]:

- to **define the objectives**, a basic comparison can be made between the future needs of the school and the ability of the current premises to support them;

- to **develop the options**, a feasibility study can be done by building professionals to look at various possible ways to meet the objectives;

- **information gathering** can then be done for each of the options, including whole-life[2] capital and revenue costs and design quality;

- to **assess and analyse the options**, scoring and weighting can be applied by setting out the options against the objectives in a table, combining financial and non-financial factors to produce a best value solution.

When the preferred option is chosen, it should provide a feasibility design that incorporates the school's vision of the future.

By developing the masterplan to feasibility design stage[3], strategic options that may have been envisaged, such a new sports hall or performing arts block, can be shown to be feasible and appropriately located. The scheme may also be usable as a 'reference design' if the entire school is covered by a contract for renewal.

Hint: Most LEAs will have a system of masterplans for schools, with various terms including Premises Development Plans, Building Development Plans and School Asset Management Plans.

1. Steps in an Option Appraisal are discussed in detail in Finding the Right Solution: a Guide to Option Appraisal, available on www.teachernet.gov.uk/amps.

2. What are 'whole-life' costs? A theoretical 'whole life cost model' can be calculated for any design, but the principle is simply to take the initial construction costs and add the running costs and replacement costs of items which form the building over a reasonable 'life time' such as 25 to 60 years.

For instance, a temporary structure may be cheaper to build than a traditional building which has a longer life time, but may be far more expensive to maintain and need to be replaced at least once in that time.

In a PFI project, the PFI provider is likely to prefer a cost that may be more expensive 'up front' but cheaper in the longer term.

3. RIBA stage B: feasibility design is a recognised early stage of the design process, as defined by the Royal Institute of British Architects. It will usually involve a fee, possibly prior to any agreed project funding. See www.architecture.com/go/Architecture/Using/Contracts.

Figure A.2: masterplan flow diagram

Masterplan, or PDP, flow diagram, showing how data on existing premises can be compared with future requirements to identify the scope of works and possible budget.

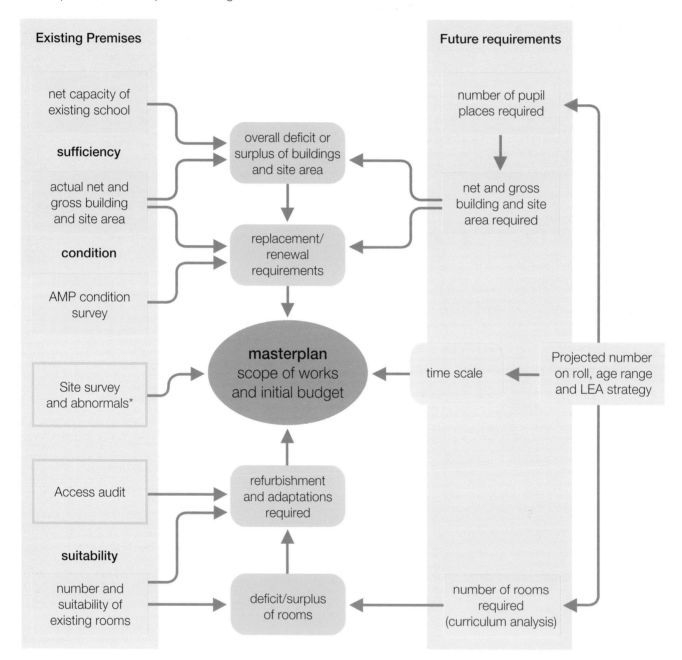

* abnormals include site conditions which would require extra funding, such as drainage, gradients, split sites, constrained site or ground contamination.

Defining the Objectives

The masterplan or PDP should be based on an objective comparison between the future premises needs of the school and the current buildings and site (as described in figure A.2 opposite). This can usually be done by the LEA or school using existing data.

The **future need** will be based on:

- the projected capacity (number of pupil places)[1], in the context of the LEA strategies and policies;

- the recommended building and site area, both net and gross, for the required age range and capacity, based on the formulae in Parts C and D;

- a curriculum analysis[2] based on the individual needs of the school's planned curriculum.

Data on the **existing buildings and site** will include:

- the Asset Management Plan (AMP) condition survey and suitability survey[3], based on a curriculum analysis as above where relevant;

- the Net Capacity[4] of current buildings, including identification of any 'non-school and support' facilities;

- other AMP sufficiency data, comprising the current net and gross building area and overall site area;

- an access audit and accessibility plan[5].

This comparison, or gap analysis, can identify the **scope of the work** required and an **initial budget** based on:

- the demolition costs of buildings that need to be removed because they are surplus or beyond economic adaptation or repair;

- new build costs[6] of further or replacement gross building area, based on the shortfall of remaining area compared to that recommended for the planned capacity;

- refurbishment costs of existing facilities related to suitability needs;

- possible acquisition or disposal of land.

Depending on the possible projected growth or change in the capacity requirements of the school, the data above can also highlight the overall **timescale** required[7].

1. The capacity should take account of the anticipated likely number of pupils at school action, school action plus or with statements for SEN, which may require specialist facilities. Any specially resourced places for pupils with specific SEN or disabilities (such as a centre for sensory impairments) will require supplementary areas (see page 49).

2. The number and type of timetabled teaching rooms required can be calculated with the assistance of a Curriculum Analysis. See **www.teachernet.gov.uk/amps** for guidance.

   A useful rule of thumb is that the number of timetabled spaces will be $N/21 + $ or $- 2$ in 11-16 schools, where N = the number of pupil places.

3. For guidance on Asset Management see **www.teachernet.gov.uk/amps**.

4. For information on net capacity assessment see **www.dfes.gov.uk/netcapacity**.

5. The Disability Discrimination Act 1995, as amended by the Special Educational Needs and Disability Act 2001, introduces Part IV 'Education' which requires schools to have Accessibility Plans to improve access for disabled pupils to the curriculum, the physical environment and information, over a three year period to March 2006. See **www.teachernet.gov.uk/wholeschool/sen/schools/accessibility/**.

6. Current costs per square metre (m²) for the region can be found in the latest DfES School Building Projects: Costs and Performance Data. Available from DfES Publications.

   Hint: overall costs including fees, site works, furniture and contingencies are likely to be at least £1500 per m².

7. For instance, the project might be planned and timed to suit the gradually increasing roll of the school and to avoid disruption as much as possible.

Figure A.3: Key headings for the brief

Introduction, encapsulating an overview and the major objectives – expressed as 'desired outcomes' rather than 'preferred solutions' – and a description of the project.

Background Information, including:

- existing school facilities and environment, including AMP data and Access Audit;
- capacity requirements and age range of the school, in line with LEA strategies and policies and anticipated community use;
- the strategic masterplan and how the project fits into it (see page 7);

- personnel, listing the key point of contact, and roles and responsibilities;
- budget, based on the likely gross area to be built and whole-life building costs;
- programme of work, including key dates to be taken into account such as examinations and holiday periods.

Vision for the School, expressing the aspirations and philosophy of the school, in the context of the School Development Plan (see page 15).

Implications for the design, as discussed in Part B, including:

- organisation and management structure of the school, and preferences for the layout and location of resources and key relationships between spaces;

- intended community use and extended school facilities;
- furniture and equipment dimensions and specification.

Design requirements, as discussed in Part B, including:

- adaptability and flexibility, ensuring the design will suit as many variations as possible in the future, including possible requirements for expansion and developments in ICT;
- access and inclusion requirements, to allow for the curriculum and informal areas to be fully accessible to pupils with SEN or disabilities;

- safety and security considerations;
- sustainability and environmental design;
- environmental performance criteria, for instance for acoustics, ventilation and daylight.

Building requirements, as discussed in Part C, including:

- gross and net area standards to be achieved;
- organisation or location policies that can affect the design;

- the schedule of accommodation (see page 29).

Site requirements, as discussed in Part D, including:

- gross and net area standards to be achieved;
- any site constraints;

- land acquisition/disposal where appropriate.

Design performance requirements, including:

- legislation and non-statutory requirements, such as relevant DfES Building Bulletins and Sport England Guidance Notes;

- room data sheets, giving detailed information about the requirements of every room;
- standards of construction (for example lifespan requirements).

Facilities Management Requirements may also be included in the brief if the project includes the running of the facilities by the contractor (such as in a PFI project).

Developing the Options

The objective comparison above will set the context, but not provide the solution. The next step is to develop the overall brief in more detail and appraise some feasibility options for the whole school based on this brief. This will require the expertise of the LEA or educational consultants and architects.

At this stage, the brief should include a schedule of accommodation, with the right number and type of teaching spaces to suit the school's curriculum, an outline of the school's organisation, ethos and aspirations and their design implications, and other key areas summarised in figure A.3 opposite.

This will ensure that the designers involved understand the context as well as the specific requirements of the work, and are given the opportunity to propose options which may offer better solutions than those initially envisaged.

The final masterplan will be based on a feasibility study, setting out a number of options which can be compared. These might include:

- a 'do nothing' option, to highlight how the current accommodation would cope with future scenarios;

- options which reorganise the existing building fabric, with different levels of replacement (and disruption);

- a total or substantially new build option[1].

All the options should be drawn up sufficiently to compare their educational advantages, likely disruption to the school, and longer term maintenance implications[2].

It is also crucial that the cost of each option is compared, both in terms of the initial capital cost and also the 'whole-life' cost over at least 25 years[3]. Costs should also include temporary rehousing of pupils if necessary, furniture and equipment (both fixed and loose)[4], and landscaping.

The masterplan is most likely to be realised through a single capital project[5] or a series of phased projects, but any smaller projects should not be at odds with the final scheme. Figures A.4 and A.5 on the next two pages show a case study example of a phased approach.

Hint: if the brief states that the final scheme should accommodate a number of rooms in a suite, the designer can investigate more options than if it states that the project is to provide a new space in a new building in a specific position, such as the courtyard.

1. This may include the use of exemplar designs. See www.teachernet.gov.uk/exemplars.

2. Other options in some schools could include accommodating the whole school on one site (if current site is split or constrained) or incorporating 'extended schools' facilities or other age ranges, with other funding.

3. see 'What are whole-life costs' on page 7.

4. Some furniture and equipment will be covered by capital funds and some by recurrent funding. This is discussed in detail in Section 3 of 'Furniture and Equipment: A Purchasing Guide', Managing School Facilities Guide 7, TSO 2000 ISBN 0 11 271092 1.

5. Such as BSF projects. The masterplan may need to allow for more than one option, for instance to allow a PFI provider to propose a completely new school where possible.

Case Study

Figure A.4: Existing: Plan of existing school buildings

In this real example, the existing school buildings provided a capacity of 750 11 to 16 places in a range of buildings. Figure A.5 shows the final master plan for the new school on the same site.

Key to both figures:
- general teaching
- science
- design and technology
- art
- music/media
- learning resources
- staff and admininistration
- storage
- halls and dining
- toilets and changing
- non-net area
- lift

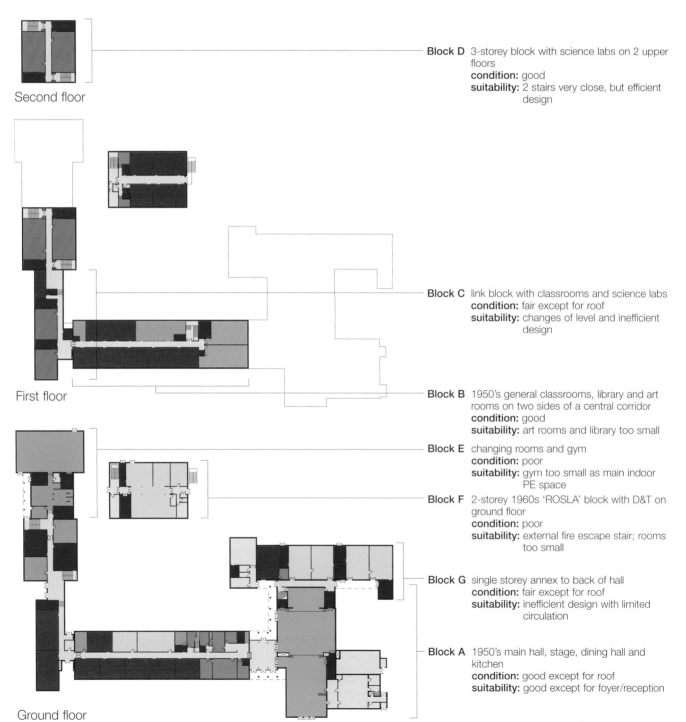

Second floor

First floor

Ground floor

Block D 3-storey block with science labs on 2 upper floors
condition: good
suitability: 2 stairs very close, but efficient design

Block C link block with classrooms and science labs
condition: fair except for roof
suitability: changes of level and inefficient design

Block B 1950's general classrooms, library and art rooms on two sides of a central corridor
condition: good
suitability: art rooms and library too small

Block E changing rooms and gym
condition: poor
suitability: gym too small as main indoor PE space

Block F 2-storey 1960s 'ROSLA' block with D&T on ground floor
condition: poor
suitability: external fire escape stair; rooms too small

Block G single storey annex to back of hall
condition: fair except for roof
suitability: inefficient design with limited circulation

Block A 1950's main hall, stage, dining hall and kitchen
condition: good except for roof
suitability: good except for foyer/reception

Case Study

Figure A.5: Masterplan: Plan of new and refurbished school buildings

The refurbished buildings were to house 900 11 to 16 places plus a sixth form. The budget was based on the costs of repairing the areas in poor condition, addressing suitability needs and adding the extra places needed. The feasibility study for the whole school considered a number of options, from 'patch and mend' of all existing buildings to complete replacement. The final design allows each department to be in a suite, whilst still having the option to expand or contract into adjacent accommodation. For site plan see page 54.

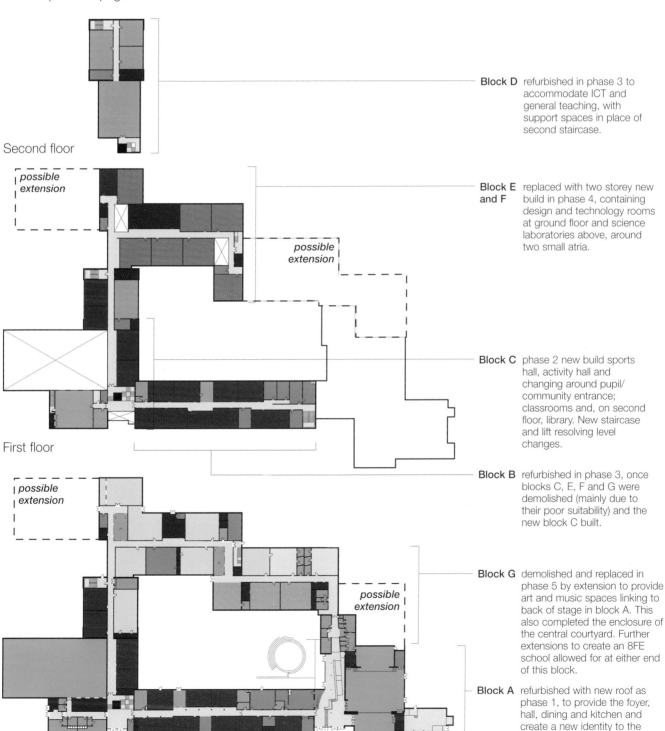

Second floor

possible extension

possible extension

First floor

possible extension

possible extension

Ground floor

Block D refurbished in phase 3 to accommodate ICT and general teaching, with support spaces in place of second staircase.

Block E and F replaced with two storey new build in phase 4, containing design and technology rooms at ground floor and science laboratories above, around two small atria.

Block C phase 2 new build sports hall, activity hall and changing around pupil/ community entrance; classrooms and, on second floor, library. New staircase and lift resolving level changes.

Block B refurbished in phase 3, once blocks C, E, F and G were demolished (mainly due to their poor suitability) and the new block C built.

Block G demolished and replaced in phase 5 by extension to provide art and music spaces linking to back of stage in block A. This also completed the enclosure of the central courtyard. Further extensions to create an 8FE school allowed for at either end of this block.

Block A refurbished with new roof as phase 1, to provide the foyer, hall, dining and kitchen and create a new identity to the school in Year 1, while block B was temporarily used for all other teaching rooms.

Case Study

Figure A.6 and A.7:

Case study school buildings before refurbishment.

Blocks D (left), C and B.

Original entrance foyer between blocks A and B.

Figure A.8 and A.9:

Case study school after refurbishment and new buildings.

New pupil entrance and sports hall in place of block C, including a double-sided lift to ensure accessibility to split levels.

New roof to hall in block A and new foyer/visitors entrance.

Part B: Design Criteria

This part highlights three types of design criteria that should be specified in the brief to ensure design quality[1]. Firstly, the 'vision' of the final school, which will affect the overarching design philosophy of any scheme. Secondly, the more practical implications for the design of the client team's preferences for:

- the organisation and management of the school, and the location of various resources;

- the size and type of furniture and equipment;

- any community use and/or extended school facilities.

And thirdly, some key design requirements crucial to the design of any school project:

- flexibility and adaptability to allow for change;

- suitability for the inclusion of pupils with special educational needs (SEN) and disabilities;

- safety and security; and

- environmental performance.

The choice: At the end of each relevant sub-heading, text in this colour highlights the choices that will affect the design.

Vision for the School

Any masterplan should ensure that the planned environment suits the identity, ethos and culture of the school. Among other overarching aspirations, the client's brief should communicate to the design team that the buildings should inspire and enhance:

- **educational performance:** opportunities to raise standards for all by offering an appropriate, adaptable and stimulating learning environment;

- **staff satisfaction:** vital for the recruitment and retention of the school's most important resource[2], it is influenced by the various aspects of the working environment as well as appropriate space for staff to rest and socialise;

- **pupil satisfaction:** affecting behaviour and self-esteem, and ultimately willingness and ability to learn;

- **community involvement:** an important way to extend the integration of the school and maximise effective access to facilities.

1. Design Quality
   The Commission for Architecture and the Built Environment (CABE), in its publication 'Better Public Buildings', has identified good design as a mix of the following attributes:

   Functionality in use, or fitness for purpose, which can be checked against the criteria in the brief;

   Build quality, including the need for whole life cost principles to be used;

   Efficiency and sustainability, ensuring the design allows buildings to be delivered on time and on cost;

   Designing in context, including the site and existing buildings, but also the need for the total design to be seen as a coherent whole;

   Aesthetic quality and the need for a non-institutional, individual character.

The Construction Industry Council (CIC) has also developed Design Quality Indicators to help to ensure quality in design. See **www.cic.org.uk/** and **www.dqi.org.uk/**. A school specific design quality indicator being developed by the DfES is due for completion in 2005.

2. This is linked to School Workforce Remodelling, which is discussed at **www.teachernet.gov.uk/wholeschool/remodelling**. See also 'Removing Barriers to Achievement: The Government Strategy for SEN 2004'. **www.teachernet.gov.uk/sen**.

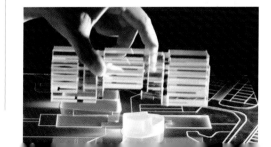

Figure B.1: Organisation Diagram

Diagram showing traditional departmental structure of a
secondary school, and the useful links between subject areas.
Various faculty options are also common which merge two or
three adjacent subjects.

Key:
- basic teaching (and storage)
- halls (and storage)
- learning resources
- staff and administration
- dining and social
- non-net area
- community use out of school hours

Not included in this diagram

Net areas
lockers for personal storage
cleaners' store

Non-net areas
pupil toilets (incl. accessible toilets)
circulation
plant
partitions

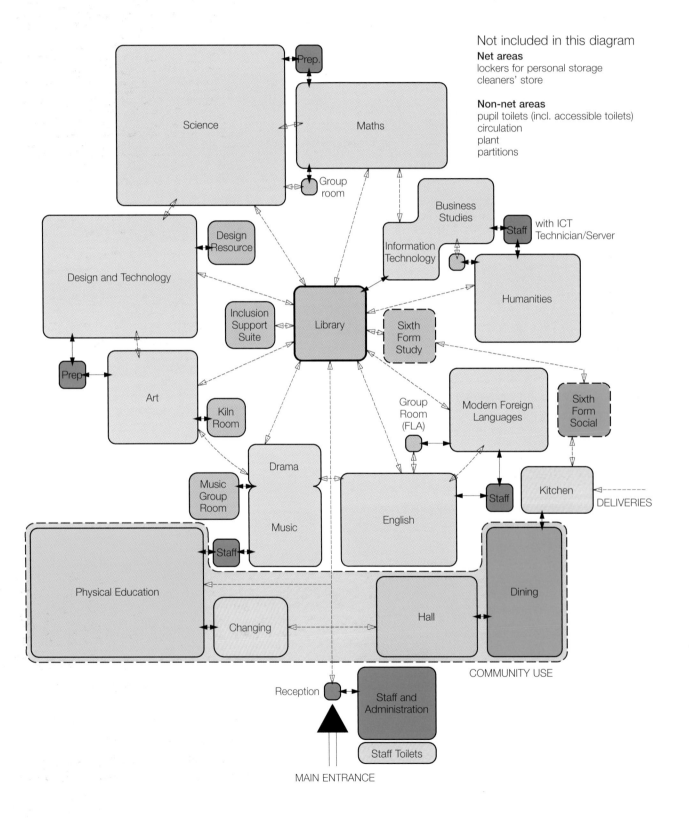

Implications for the Design

At a more practical level, a number of key decisions about the organisation, management and pastoral support systems of the school can have major implications for the layout of the site, particularly where there are site constraints, or where existing buildings are suitable but not ideally placed or orientated.

It is therefore important that the brief clearly sets out the school's preferences for the following issues, taking into account the likely future direction as far as possible.

Organisation

The school may prefer a departmental structure (as shown in figure B.1 opposite), larger faculties or other groupings[1]. Some schools prefer an upper and lower school structure, particularly where there are split sites. Similarly, sixth form accommodation may be partially or significantly separate.

Alternative options for registration and pastoral care are becoming more common, including mixed age registration groups, 'house' systems (particularly in larger schools) or 'schools within schools'[2].

These alternatives can involve all but the most specialist teaching spaces (such as design and technology rooms and halls) being provided in various points around the school site, dispersed resources and social areas, and less movement around the school. However, this can also involve more duplication of facilities and higher numbers of support staff.

Location Policies: Central or Local Resources?

Various types of resources may be deliberately centralised, with the advantage of easy access to support staff and specialist equipment. Alternatively, they may be spread around the school, with the advantage of easy access to departments or faculties and shorter travel distances. This will clearly have an effect on the final design.

The choice: The brief should specify the location policy under each category of space, as discussed in similar boxes in Part C, covering ICT, examinations, learning resources, staff accommodation, personal storage and dining facilities.

1. Variations 5 to 7 of the secondary school exemplar design brief are examples of these organisational options. Go to www.teachernet.gov.uk/exemplars and find 'secondary exemplar design brief annexe 1' for schedules of accommodation.

2. Schools within schools are considered in the exemplar designs compendium Exemplar Designs: concepts and ideas, page 13. See www.teachernet.gov.uk/exemplars for a pdf version or order by emailing dfes@prologistics.co.uk.

Hint: Although it may seem sensible to house departments in different blocks, it may be less easy to expand or contract a department if it is in a separate block or wing that exactly suits its initial requirements.

Time Management

The way that the school day is timetabled can significantly affect the design. Staggered timetables can reduce the demand for area – from half the school being able to access dining facilities while the other half is in lessons[1], to whole year groups, such as the sixth form, being taught at different times of the day and reducing the demand for timetabled teaching spaces.

Using Technology

Classrooms may be furnished for registration groups of 30 or more, but may normally be used for much smaller teaching groups. More space can be made available within each room by:

- using swipe cards for registration and avoiding registration classes; or

- using laboratories with appropriate furniture and services 'cut-off' for registration/pastoral groups.

ICT and interactive whiteboards may allow more subjects to be taught in the same classroom and reduce pupil movement and crowded circulation areas, particularly in multi-storey buildings.

Furniture and Equipment

Careful consideration of the activities required in each room should identify the items of furniture and equipment needed, which can then inform a number of layouts. To avoid compromises, the preferred layout options and size of furniture[2] should be drawn within the plan of the room to ensure the dimensions and size are sufficient.

If the brief covers furniture and equipment, strength and stability should be assured by using relevant standards. It is also important to consider ergonomics. Care must be taken to ensure that the chairs and tables provided are compatible heights and suitable for pupils using them[3].

The choice: The options described on this page can mean that some space can be used more effectively. For instance, some teaching rooms can be furnished for group sizes smaller than 30, allowing more space for larger tables or more layout options.

1. If this option is to be available, the dining and social facilities should be positioned such that their use cannot disturb pupils in quiet lessons or study.

   Hint: If using a 'split lunch' system, it may be easier to have a minority of pupils eating lunch at any one time: this can make the prevailing activity in the school quiet work, rather than noisy social activities, at all times, as well as reducing queues.

2. Tables of 600mm x 1200mm, typical in schools today, are appropriate in 'small' classrooms with an area in zone B on page 30. To allow more table top space for the older age groups and for portable ICT in the classroom, larger tables of 700mm x 1400mm may be more useful (particularly where the room is predominantly for the sixth form or KS4), and these will fit in 'standard' classrooms in zone C on page 30.

   With either size of tables, room areas at the top of the zone will offer more options for variations in layout and circulation space around tables than the bottom of the zone. To allow for the varying needs of disabled pupils, the examples above also allow for a 700mm x 1400mm height adjustable table, located for easy access and circulation.

3. Both ergonomics and strength and stability standards for furniture are referred to in 'Furniture and Equipment: A Purchasing Guide', Managing School Facilities Guide 7, TSO 2000 ISBN 0 11 271092 1

Extended School Facilities

Any mainstream secondary school can provide extended school[1] activities and services, outside the school day, to help meet the needs of its pupils, their families and the wider community. Some schools may provide more extensive provision for non-school use during the school day.

Extended school facilities will generally fall into one of three levels of provision:

- *access to school facilities by the wider local community* beyond the school day should be available in any school, addressed through the design and management of the building and the provision listed above;

- *flexible multi-use areas for use by others* within the school during the school day, such as a parent/community room or SEN facilities that may also be used for community health care, may be accommodated within the 'float' area or some 'supplementary area' funded by the LEA;

- *major areas for dedicated non-educational services* would require supplementary areas (see page 49) funded through the joining up of other funding streams, such as Sure Start or Primary Care Trusts.

The location of any facilities that will be used by the community should be carefully considered, taking into account access, security, child protection and parking.

Linked Provision

Some facilities may be accessed nearby, such as a swimming pool or specialist vocational resources. The brief should identify the implications of any such linked provision.

1. For further information on extended schools, see www.teachernet.gov.uk/wholeschool/extended schools.

Hint: Use by the community can affect VAT charged for building projects in Voluntary Aided schools and others where funding is not via the LEA.

Part B: Design Criteria

Shared Community Use

The level, frequency and likely timing of community use should be assessed early in the briefing process, in conjunction with the Local Authority's strategy for sports and leisure amenities[1].

Shared spaces are likely to include the main hall or performance space and its ancillary facilities, and sports facilities, both indoor and outdoor. Links with adult learning provision and other local schools may also lead to shared use of some specialist learning spaces such as ICT suites or art and drama facilities. The design should allow these parts of the school to be open and heated while others are closed and secure.

Facilities which will encourage community use outside the school day, and are allowed for within the recommended gross area (page 25), include:

- alternative 'reception' facilities and access for out-of-hours use;

- sports hall, activity studio and changing facilities suitable for public use;

- accessible toilets and lockers for use by adult visitors;

- a community office and storage spaces separate from those used by the school;

- environmental learning areas available to be managed in partnership with specialist groups and the local community.

Curriculum Opportunities

The whole site development, or the process of change involved in upgrading an existing school, is a major opportunity for pupils to study and experience citizenship and education for sustainable development first hand. This can include conflict resolution and the balancing of financial, social, practical and environmental criteria.

The brief should highlight the need for designers, contractors and the school to take advantage of this opportunity, in line with the requirements of the DfES Action Plan for Sustainable Development in Education and Skills[2].

1. Refer to Sport England Technical Guidance Notes 'Village and Community Halls', 'Access for Disabled People' and 'Designing Space for Sports and Arts'. See www.sportengland.org/resources /resource_downloads.shtml.

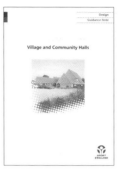 

Hint: Shared use can affect the requirements for emergency lighting and fire escape provision to suit public use. Community use during the school day can increase the demand for car parking.

© Learning Through Landscapes

2. School Works and Learning through Landscapes have direct experience in how to plan and manage this type of pupil involvement. See www.school-works.org and www.ltl.org.uk.

Key Design Requirements

The following issues should be identified as essential in the brief for any project.

Flexibility and Adaptability

The flexibility to allow for change must be a key design requirement. Whatever layout is preferred, it must be adaptable to allow for future changes, for instance for different timetable models to be adopted. What is suitable now will, as often as not, need to be changed in a few years.

Flexibility is needed to allow for day to day change of use, such as accommodating different teaching arrangements in a classroom through movable furniture[1] and portable ICT (see page 33).

Adaptability is needed to allow for long-term changes such as developments in the 14 to 19 curriculum or the implications of evolving ICT. The consequences for the school of the future are difficult to predict, but room sizes may need to change (to match varying group sizes) and servicing requirements may alter (see page 32).

Avoiding fixed furniture as much as possible and limiting the range allows flexibility. Furniture can also provide flexibility by performing a number of functions, although this must be offset with the need for simple products which are not difficult to repair or replace (see page 18).

It is important to be clear what needs to be adaptable (for instance internal walls being able to be removed and rebuilt without affecting the structure or major services) and what should be flexible for more frequent change. For instance, sliding/folding doors can often be underused and ineffective, but may be useful to allow rooms to change size to match unpredictable sixth form group sizes or to allow for an examination space[2].

1. The pictures above show how the furniture layout of a standard classroom can be rearranged to suit different learning styles: from Building Bulletin 92: Modern Foreign Languages: A Design Guide TSO 2000. ISBN 0 11 271093 x.

2. See exemplar design secondary school brief at www.teachernet.gov.uk/exemplars.

Access and Inclusion

Access and inclusion must be allowed for in the design, reflecting the Government's commitment to promoting inclusion of pupils with special educational needs (SEN) and disabilities into mainstream schools. This means that such pupils should be able to have access to the whole curriculum and participate in school life[1].

Particular attention should be given to:

- appropriate space for pupil support, whether educational (for instance through small group rooms), therapeutic, social or medical;

- an easily understood layout and suitable use of colour and good signage;

- good quality acoustics and lighting[2] (and perhaps a higher specification in specialist areas);

- access designed for all to information, the curriculum and the physical environment[3] (for instance including both a ramp and steps where there is a small change of level[4]).

Part C recommends minimum sizes for teaching spaces that allow for pupils with SEN and disabilities and assistants. The range of facilities allowed for within the recommended gross area (page 25), to ensure an inclusive school, also include:

- SEN resource base (see page 39);

- multi-purpose small group rooms for specialist teaching and pupil support;

- office space, medical and therapy rooms for peripatetic staff and health professionals;

- meeting rooms for parents and carers;

- storage space for educational and mobility equipment;

- accessible toilets and hygiene facilities for assisted use;

- suitably wide corridors (see page 47).

In some schools, very high numbers or increased needs of pupils with SEN and disabilities will require additional specialist SEN resourced provision (in supplementary area, page 49). Alternatively, there may be a co-located special school for pupils with complex needs, which will also have implications for the mainstream school.

1. Typically, pupils with speech, language and communication needs, specific learning difficulties, moderate learning difficulties, sensory impairments physical disabilities and medical needs will, as far as possible, be included in most mainstream schools. Refer to BB77 Designing for SEN: Special Schools, to be updated 2004.

2. See BB90: Lighting Design for Schools TSO 1999. ISBN 0 11 271041 7; and BB87: Guidelines for Environmental Design in Schools, May 2003 web version, at: **www.teachernet.gov.uk/energy** and BB93: Acoustics in Schools at: **www.teachernet.gov.uk/acoustics**.

3. As defined in The DfES Guidance Note: Accessible Schools: planning to increase access to schools for disabled pupils LEA/0168/2002 **www.teachernet.gov.uk/sen**. For details of access requirements refer to Building Regulations Approved Document M, 2004 and BS 8300.

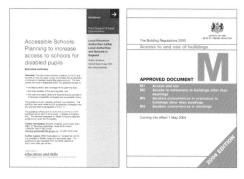

4. Note that changes of level of one step only are not permitted in Approved Document M (above), either internally or externally.

Safety and Security

Safety and security[1] are over-arching issues, which should be considered in conjunction with requirements for greater community access. Security is as much about creating a feeling of a secure, organised, safe environment, as it is about the specifics of surveillance and supervision of access. Particular attention needs to be given to:

- access control, for instance to ensure visitors can be shown to an interview room from reception, but cannot enter the school without permission;

- securing the building 'envelope': walls and roofs, but particularly windows and doors;

- having clearly defined site boundaries, using appropriate fencing and/or planting;

- electronic measures, such as intruder alarms;

- a health and safety audit of the design to ensure it is appropriate for adults and pupils with special needs or disabilities.

Environmental Performance

The brief should specify sustainable and environmental design such that a BREEAM rating[2] of good, very good or excellent is achieved. The choice will have cost implications, both in the short and long term, so the rating set in the brief should be considered carefully.

To ensure a reasonable level of sustainability, BREEAM considers a wide range of factors, including site security, community use and site selection, alongside better known environmental issues such as energy efficiency, minimising waste and using appropriate materials.

Environmental performance criteria are also crucial, particularly for acoustics, heating, ventilation and daylight. Many of these are now statutory and are vital to ensure comfortable, suitable teaching space. Acoustic and energy calculations must be provided for all designs[3].

1. See Managing School Facilities Guide 4, *Improving Security in Schools*. TSO 1996. ISBN 0 11 270916 8. Single copies available to schools from DfES Publications free of charge. Otherwise from TSO.

2. The Building Research Establishment Environmental Assessment Method (BREEAM) for schools (available by 2005) will assist in guiding the design, and should be used to assess the environmental performance of new designs. See www.bre.co.uk/breeam. See also BB87 at www.teachernet.gov.uk/energy and BB93 at www.teachernet.gov.uk/acoustics.

3. Section 1.2 of Building Bulletin 93 (above) explains how the designer must demonstrate compliance to the Building Control Body, to comply with the Building Regulations.

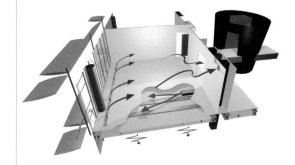

Figure C.1: gross and net area defined

Supplementary net area, which will be separately funded, should be added to the total net area to ensure the non-net area is increased proportionally.

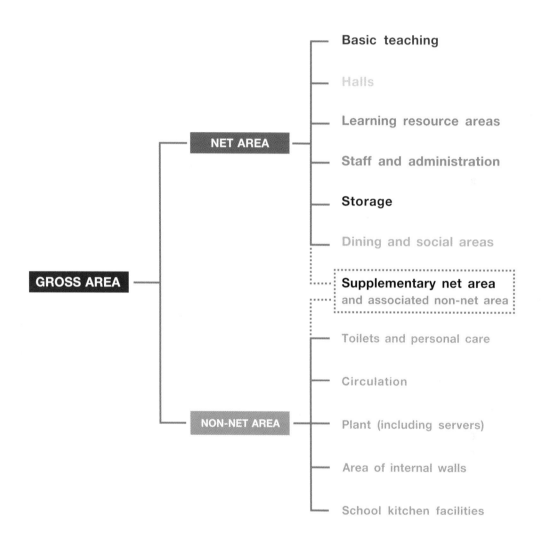

Part C: The Buildings

Setting out the appropriate areas for the different components of the school buildings requires careful and methodical discussion by the briefing team. This part sets out a clear and simple process for establishing the areas required for the accommodation schedule.

Gross Area of Buildings

Area recommendations for buildings are separated into two categories:

- *net area*, or usable area, which can be accurately calculated from the formulae in appendix 3 and in figures C.2 and C.3; plus any agreed supplementary net area; and

- *non-net area*, such as circulation, which will be more variable depending on the design, the configuration of existing buildings and site constraints, but will generally increase in proportion to the net area.

The total of these categories gives the gross area of the buildings[1], as described in figure C.1 opposite.

The gross area required will depend on the design and layout of buildings. Generally, the gross area of new buildings may vary between 140% and 145% of the net area (such that the net is 69% to 71.5% of the gross), depending on the layout and type of site[2]. In existing buildings, this may rise to as much as 150%. In new buildings, the gross area will need to be at least 140% of the net area unless compromises are made in the provision of circulation space[3].

The total net area required by an inclusive community school should not normally need to exceed the recommended net area for the number of pupil places and age range of the school.

Further **supplementary net area**, and a proportional increase in non-net area, may be needed if there are specially resourced non-school or support functions on the school site (as discussed on page 49).

Decisions about any facilities to be provided within supplementary net area will vary widely due to specific local needs and other joined up funding streams[4].

Hint: It is important to realise that it will be the budget, rather than the gross area, which will be the determining constraint on the project. So the gross area could be larger than that recommended, as long as it can be achieved within the budget allocated.

1. The gross area is measured to the internal face of external walls in all parts of all buildings on the school site(s) that are intended to be secure and weather-tight, except residential or farm buildings in use as such, or buildings condemned by the LEA as structurally unsafe.

2. The budget for new schools should allow for a gross area that is around 142.5% of the recommended net area.

3. In some cases, such as sloping sites, this may need to increase.

4. It is important that the budget allows for any supplementary area that is required over and above the recommended net area.

Figure C.2: 11-16 net and gross area

Graphs showing recommended areas for total net and gross area, and categories of net area in 11 to 16 schools. Note that the areas in the top graph are at a different scale to those in the lower graph (so that the basic teaching area, zone P, is usually more than all the other areas put together).

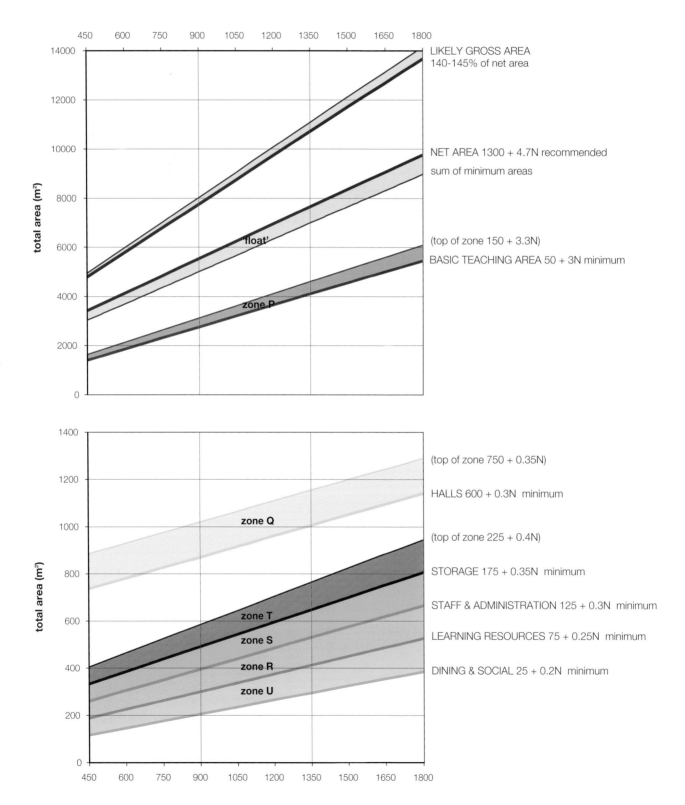

number of 11-16 pupil places (N)

Net Area of Buildings

The net area[1] is made up of rooms within the six categories of space listed below, plus any supplementary net areas for non-school or support functions, as discussed above. In diagram C.2 opposite, the likely areas of each category for 11 to 16 schools are shown as zones P to U.

- basic teaching area   (zone P);
- halls   (zone Q);
- learning resource areas   (zone R);
- staff and administration   (zone S);
- storage   (zone T);
- dining and social   (zone U).

The bottom of each zone, which can be calculated using the formulae shown, represents the minimum recommended area for that category of space.

The total area for each of these categories should be at least the minimum recommended in this bulletin (i.e. the bottom of the zone). If any of the individual categories are insufficient for the site[2] (even if the total net area is enough) this is likely to compromise the best use of the buildings.

An area greater than the minimum but within the zone will usually be required for each category. The overall recommended net and gross area allows for the area of each category of space to average around the middle of each zone, through the provision of some 'float'[3]. In practice, the float can be used to provide extra accommodation where it is most needed by each school: for instance, it could be used for an extra dance studio, further staff accommodation or a larger library.

Funding for major school projects[4] will generally be based on the recommended gross area (plus any agreed supplementary areas), and this will clearly **not** be sufficient for all categories of space to be at the top of each zone – decisions have to be made against the particular priorities of the school (see Part B).

1. The net area includes all spaces in the gross area of buildings, except toilets, washrooms and showers (and lobbies to them, including changing rooms), plant areas such as boiler rooms, circulation space, school kitchens and the area taken up by internal walls.

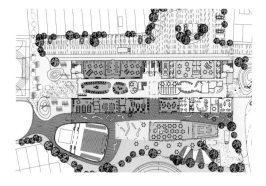

2. split sites (where a significant part of the school is provided on each site) will generally need to use the full formulae for each site, except for halls, to allow for the replication of resources required.

3. What is the float? When you add together the recommended minimum area of each category of space, the total will be around 8 to 11% less than the recommended standard for the total net area. This difference provides the 'float' which can be used to enhance some areas, depending on the priorities of the school.

4. Such as within the Building Schools for the Future programme.

Figure C.3: post-16 net and gross areas

Graphs showing recommended areas for total additional net and gross area, and categories of net area, in sixth forms in secondary schools. Note that the areas in the top graph are at a different scale to those in the lower graph (like figure C.2).

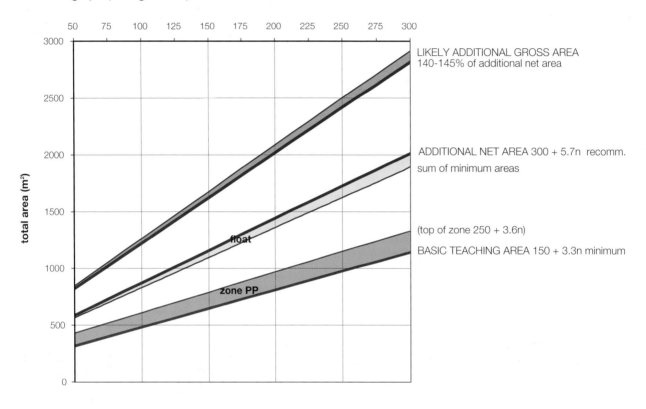

LIKELY ADDITIONAL GROSS AREA
140-145% of additional net area

ADDITIONAL NET AREA 300 + 5.7n recomm.

sum of minimum areas

(top of zone 250 + 3.6n)
BASIC TEACHING AREA 150 + 3.3n minimum

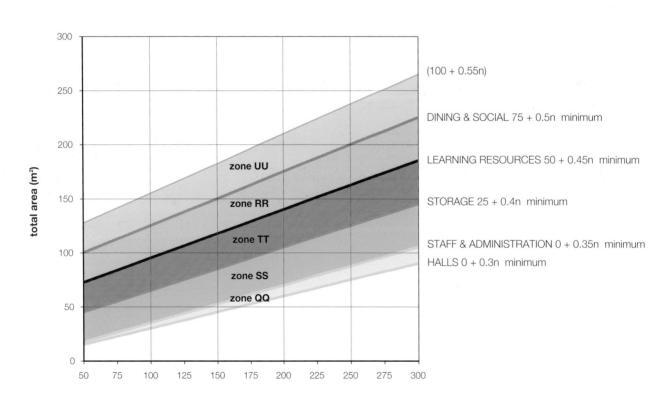

(100 + 0.55n)

DINING & SOCIAL 75 + 0.5n minimum

LEARNING RESOURCES 50 + 0.45n minimum

STORAGE 25 + 0.4n minimum

STAFF & ADMINISTRATION 0 + 0.35n minimum

HALLS 0 + 0.3n minimum

number of 16-19 pupil places (n)

The graphs in figure C.3 opposite show zones PP to UU representing the recommended area for the six categories of space, as discussed above, for additional sixth forms in secondary schools.

Schedule of Accommodation

A core part of any brief will be the schedule of accommodation to be provided. A schedule for the whole school will include spaces in all of the six categories of space.

This bulletin includes two sets of example schedules that can be used as a starting point for developing a schedule individual to the school.

- In appendix 2, schedules for four sizes of 11 to 16 school and two sizes of additional sixth form are listed in order of the six categories[1].

- In appendix 3, different schedules are shown for the same sized school, showing a number of possible variations. These are listed by department, which may be a more accessible format, but mixes categories[2].

Whichever format is used, the total of each category of net area should be totalled and compared to the minimum recommended standard.

The next few pages give some guidance on the spaces required within each category. Each category:

- **must** include spaces required by regulation;
- **should** include spaces or areas in line with best practice and non-statutory guidance;
- **may** include other spaces where appropriate to the school's priorities or preferences.

The number and type of timetabled teaching spaces, within the basic teaching area and halls area, will depend on the demands of each school's curriculum. These in turn will determine the type of teaching storage required and some learning resource areas.

The number of each type of teaching space will usually only vary from those used in appendix 2 by plus or minus one, but the final brief should be based on a 'curriculum analysis' specific to the individual school's demands[3].

Hint: bear in mind that these are guidelines. The specific objectives of each school should be considered when making decisions about how much area to allocate to each activity – for instance, taking account of its specialism.

1. These schedules, at the back of this book, are not intended to be prescriptive, but to indicate one of a number of possible sets of spaces, based on a typical curriculum and organisation.

2. Similar curriculum based variations for an 1150 place 11-18 school can be found in the exemplar design brief variations 8 and 9. See www.teachernet.gov.uk/exemplars: secondary brief annex 2.

3. The number and type of timetabled teaching rooms required can be calculated with the assistance of a curriculum analysis. See www.teachernet.gov.uk/amps for guidance.

A useful rule of thumb is that the number of timetabled spaces will be N/21 + or – 2 in 11-16 schools, where N = the number on roll.

Figure C.4: size of teaching spaces

Graph showing zones of recommended area for teaching spaces within the basic teaching area. The bottom of each zone represents the minimum size recommended for the group size, and can be calculated using the formulae shown.

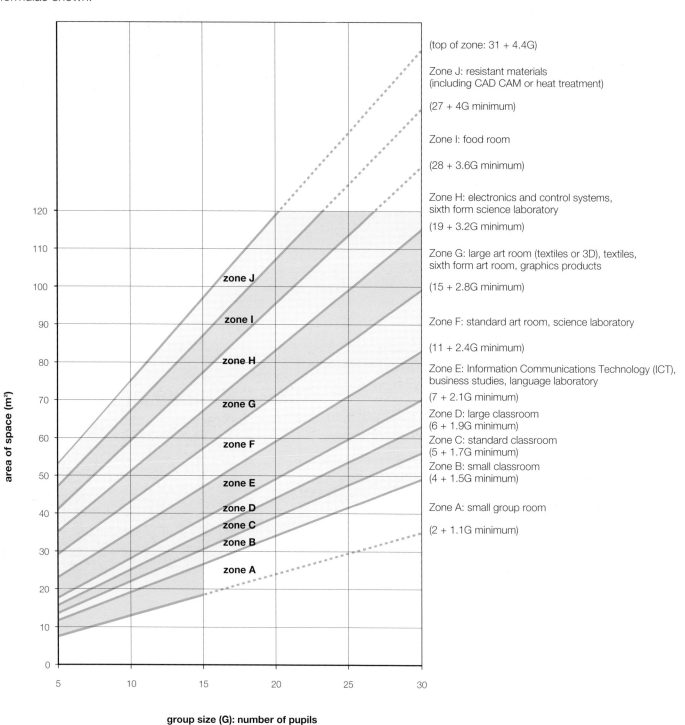

(top of zone: 31 + 4.4G)

Zone J: resistant materials
(including CAD CAM or heat treatment)

(27 + 4G minimum)

Zone I: food room

(28 + 3.6G minimum)

Zone H: electronics and control systems, sixth form science laboratory

(19 + 3.2G minimum)

Zone G: large art room (textiles or 3D), textiles, sixth form art room, graphics products

(15 + 2.8G minimum)

Zone F: standard art room, science laboratory

(11 + 2.4G minimum)

Zone E: Information Communications Technology (ICT), business studies, language laboratory

(7 + 2.1G minimum)

Zone D: large classroom
(6 + 1.9G minimum)

Zone C: standard classroom
(5 + 1.7G minimum)

Zone B: small classroom
(4 + 1.5G minimum)

Zone A: small group room

(2 + 1.1G minimum)

area of space (m²)

group size (G): number of pupils

Basic Teaching Area

Basic teaching area comprises all timetabled teaching rooms except halls (within zones P and PP), and should include the following types of space:

- *General teaching classrooms:* at least three for every 150 pupil places.

- *Practical areas:* at least one science laboratory for every 150 pupils and usually at least one design and technology space or art room for every 150 pupils;

- *'Performance spaces':* at least one music, drama or media space in the school (dance and PE are covered under halls on page 37).

It may also include other timetabled rooms for ICT, business or specific vocational studies, or a multi-gym.

The graph opposite (figure C.4) gives area guidance for individual teaching spaces within the basic teaching area, depending on the maximum group size. A curriculum analysis can identify the maximum group size in each subject[1]. However, to allow for a flexible set of spaces, the general rule used in the example schedules is to use a maximum group size of 30 for all spaces except design and technology (based instead on 20) and any spaces used specifically for the sixth form, such as seminar rooms.

This maximum may only be needed for some groups and for registration. In the same typical model, class sizes usually average 25 to 27 in Key Stage 3 and less in Key Stage 4 and the sixth form, so some rooms may not need to accommodate as many as 30 unless used for registration (see page 18), while a few may need to accommodate more. This is important to remember when considering how the full curriculum can best be accessed by all pupils, including those requiring assistants or mobility equipment.

The minimum size for each space, represented by the formulae at the bottom of the relevant zone, generally allows for one wheelchair user, assistants, and an increasing amount of portable ICT equipment (including projectors)[2]. However, it does not allow for any significant storage in furniture or coat and bag racks, as this is allowed for under the storage category.

Space sizes used in the example schedules in Appendices 2 and 3 are generally in the middle of the relevant zone, to allow for further flexibility of furniture layouts and more wheelchair users or assistants.

1. The maximum group size may be smaller than 30 because the year group is taught in more groups, or it is only an optional subject and options are taught in smaller groups. Maximum group sizes in design and technology are generally recommended to be 20.

2. More detailed information on individual spaces should be identified in Room Data Sheets such as those on the web. See **www.teachernet.gov.uk/ exemplars**, Secondary Exemplar Design Brief Annex.

© Learning Through Landscapes

Part C: The Buildings

31

Figure C.5: six classroom 'cluster' options

The diagrams below indicate how a 'cluster' configuration of two adaptable areas of 180m², plus ancillary space, on either side of a circulation route or shared resource area, can suit a variety of provision for different schools and for future learning options.

Key:

- basic teaching
- staff workroom
- small group room
- store

* number of computer workstations (notional)

Note: corridor shown at 2.1m wide for diagrams, but other configurations may be preferred.

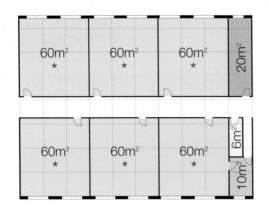

Six 60m² classrooms with some portable ICT in each.

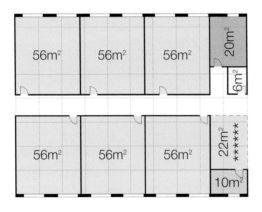

Six 56m² classrooms plus an ICT 'cluster' for up to 12 computers.

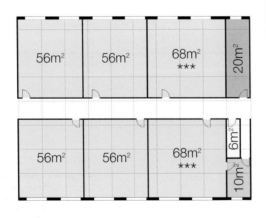

Four 56m² classrooms and two 68m² classrooms, large enough for ICT workstations.

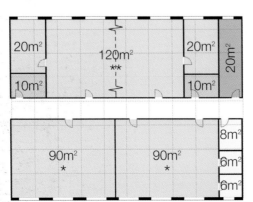

Longer term option using the same adaptability to create 90m² practical rooms or a large area for team teaching with adjacent small group rooms. This may have implications for the capacity of the school.

General Teaching Spaces

Almost half the subjects taught in secondary schools are 'general teaching', normally requiring standard classrooms. These include English, mathematics, modern foreign languages[1], history, geography, religious education, general studies and personal, health and social education (citizenship).

In new schools these should all be at least standard classrooms (zone C in figure C.4) to ensure each has sufficient room for wheelchair users and assistants, as well as accommodating computers for up to 60% of the maximum group[2]. Ideally, this can be within a cluster configuration as shown in figure C.5 (opposite), allowing for future adaptability[3].

In existing buildings, some may be small classrooms (zone B), but there should be at least one standard classroom in each department, and alternative facilities for untimetabled access for ICT (see page 39). A few large classrooms (zone D) can be useful to allow further activities such as map work or role play.

ICT Rooms

In addition to increasing portable ICT, there is likely to continue to be a need for one or two specialist ICT rooms (zone E in figure C.4), equipped with personal computers for each workstation, to teach computing as a subject, or to accommodate a language laboratory. However, the demand for further untimetabled ICT rooms or clusters, for other subjects to use as a bookable resource, is likely to diminish as laptop or tablet computers become more common[4].

Rooms in zone E may also be appropriate for business studies (perhaps with a smaller maximum group size) or non-practical vocational courses.

ICT location policy: in the future, ICT facilities used in subjects other than ICT are likely to be mainly in classrooms, perhaps using advances in portable, wireless technology. However, schools may prefer current trends of specialist ICT rooms for timetabled classes, one larger room in each department having ICT, or departmental clusters with access for everyone. Part of the 'float' area should be used to provide any of these options, but each will impact on the design.

1. Refer to BB92: Modern Foreign Languages Accommodation: A Design Guide TSO 2000. ISBN 0 11 271093 x

2. Assuming the use of some tables of 1400 x 700, suitable for laptop or flat screen computers, and space for an adjustable height table and specialist equipment for a pupil with SEN or disabilities.

3. In the schedules in appendix 2, all general teaching classrooms are at least 56m² (the minimum in zone C for a group of 30), but a further 4m² is included to allow for larger classrooms or other variations as in figure C.5. See also exemplar designs compendium pages 16 and 17 at **www.teachernet.gov.uk/exemplars**.

4. In the exemplar design brief, the only specific ICT facility is two ICT rooms, on the basis that, at 59m², all general teaching classrooms are large enough to accommodate personal computers at up to half of the workstations, or laptops or tablets at all of them. For further information on ICT in schools see the British Educational Communications and Technology Agency (Becta) at **www.ictadvice.org.uk**

Figure C.6: area requirements for typical group sizes

The table below gives a quick reference summary of areas for different general, practical and performance teaching rooms for three maximum group sizes, based on the middle of the zones in figure C.4. However, this will vary depending on the activities to be accommodated. It is important for the design/briefing team to exercise judgement based on the particular needs of their school, using the detailed guidance in the Building Bulletins referred to in the text.

Space type	Recommended area (m²) according to group size			
	for 20	for 25	for 30	zone
small classroom	35	43	51	B
standard classroom/seminar room	43	51	60	C
large classroom	48	57	66	D
ICT room or business studies	55	66	77	E
language laboratory	55	66	77	E
science laboratory KS3/4		77	90	F
sixth form science laboratory	90	105		H
general art room for KS3/4		77	90	F
large art room (textiles or 3D)		90	105	G
sixth form art room	77	90		G
textiles room	85			H
graphic products	85			H
electronics and control systems	90			H
resistant materials	112			J
resistant materials/engineering	116			J
food room	101			I
music classroom		57	67	D
music recital room		77	90	F
drama/audio-visual studio		77	90	F

Practical Teaching Spaces

Practically-based subjects, including science[1], design and technology[2], art[3] and some vocational courses require a range of specialist teaching spaces. These fall into two types[4]:

- 'light practical' (zones E to H) with water, drainage and perhaps gas services and resistant finishes; and

- 'heavy practical' (zones I and J) with fixed machines (such as lathes or cookers), very resistant finishes, heavy electrical loads and usually a need for some specialist extraction.

Figure C.6 shows typical areas in the middle of the relevant zones. Light practical spaces can often be accommodated in similar clusters to general teaching (as in figure C.5), although all but science laboratories, which will be serviced by a central preparation room, will need at least one accessible 'walk-in' store accessed from the room.

Heavy practical rooms tend to be large and, because of the configuration of furniture and equipment, generally need to be at least 8m wide.

Performance Teaching Spaces

Music[5], drama and media studies will require spaces with appropriate acoustic properties, and blackout facilities where necessary, with access to a hall for performances to audiences larger than the class group. Dance would be taught in spaces in the halls category.

These spaces may also be suitable and popular for community use and this should be considered when specifying their location and other requirements[6].

Support Spaces

Access to support spaces is also important, covered under learning resource areas on page 39. This is particularly true in music, where a class group should be able to break into four or five smaller groups in small group/practice rooms and an ensemble room.

1. see BB80: Science Accommodation in Secondary Schools: A Design Guide. TSO revised 2004. ISBN 0 11 271039 5

2. see BB81: Design and Technology Accommodation in Secondary Schools: A Design Guide. TSO revised 2004. ISBN 0 11 271039 5

3. see BB89: Art Accommodation in Secondary Schools. TSO 1998. ISBN 0 11 271029 8

4. These types also match net capacity definitions, as in Assessing the Net Capacity of Schools DfES/0739/2001 REV. See www.dfes.gov.uk/netcapacity.

5. see BB86: Music Accommodation in Secondary Schools. TSO 1997. ISBN 0 11 271002 6

6. Refer to Sport England Technical Guidance Notes and 'Designing Space for Sports and Arts'. See www.sportengland.org/index/get_resources/resource_downloads.htm.

Graph showing recommended area for halls for any secondary school, including those with sixth forms. Lower broken line indicates area needed for three out of five year groups in an 11 to 16 school to assemble at one time, which may be most suitable in larger schools. The broken line above this indicates the area needed for the whole school to assemble: equivalent to 0.3m² per pupil.

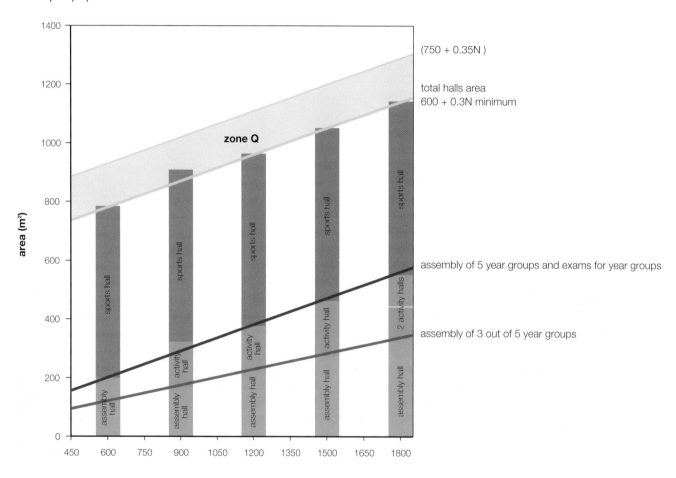

number of 11-18 pupil places (N)

Halls

Halls are large spaces[1] that have particular height, finish and acoustic criteria, depending on their use.

In new schools over 450 places[2], the total area (zone Q for any secondary school) should include:

- a main hall sufficient for assemblies of at least half the school at one time, examinations, public performances, parents' evenings and community events;

- a 'four-court' sports hall, which should be designed to Sport England's specifications, including the critical minimum dimensions for four badminton courts of 18m x 33m x 7.6m high[3];

- an activity studio of at least 145m^2, with a minimum internal width of 10m and height of 3.5m and a sprung floor[4], for some gymnastic activities, dance[5] and examinations if required.

In existing schools, there should generally be at least three large spaces totalling a similar area and volume as those described above.

The graph opposite (figure C.7) shows how these spaces could fit within the recommended zone for halls in secondary schools. In smaller schools, decisions need to be made as to the use of the 'float' area (see page 27), which may be used to provide an activity studio. The hall or sports hall may accommodate gymnastics and dance if it has a sprung floor and extra space for wall-hung equipment, if the demand for indoor PE spaces can be satisfied by two spaces and if other subjects such as drama have their own teaching space.

The minimum recommended area (600m^2 + 0.3m^2 per pupil place) allows for any school to have a sports hall or equivalent that need not be used for examinations, as the remaining area will be sufficient for a full year group and a fifth of any sixth form to sit an examination[6]. This relies on the main hall being sufficiently separate to the main school and circulation routes to avoid any disturbance, but allows full use of the sports hall by the PE department and ensures that this space is not required for activities that are not planned for in the normal specification[7].

Examinations location policy: the briefing team should consider carefully the implications of examinations and their preferred location, and the impact on the location and specification of halls, as well as storage.

1. Generally over 150m^3, with high ceilings. See net capacity guidance at **www.dfes.gov.uk/netcapacity**.

2. Schools with below 450 pupil places may require community use and funding to justify a four-court sports hall, although the area formula allows for it.

3. A larger area may be required for some uses. See Sport England Guidance Notes 'Sports Halls: Sizes and Layouts' (ISBN 1 86078 108 X) and 'Sports Halls: Design' (ISBN 1 86078 094 6).

4. To comply with BS7044 part 4.

5. Further guidance on dance studios is available from the National Dance Teachers Association. See **www.ndta.org.uk**.

6. This area is also equivalent to the area of the full compliment of pupils standing in an assembly, so if it is all in one space (or linked spaces), a full assembly can also be achieved without using the sports hall.

7. The recommended specification of the sports hall will be based on a maximum group of 60 pupils plus staff, involved in physical activities. See Room Data Sheets at **www.teachernet.gov.uk/exemplars**. Secondary Exemplar Design Brief Annex 4.

Figure C.8: total area of learning resources

Graph showing recommended learning resource area for 11 to
16 schools (zone R) and 11 to 18 schools with a typically sized
sixth form (based on a proportional use of zone RR). It also
shows the minimum recommended area for a single library
resource centre for any secondary school. The higher end of the
range could apply to a school with decentralised resource
facilities, local ICT clusters and a variety of specialist support
spaces.

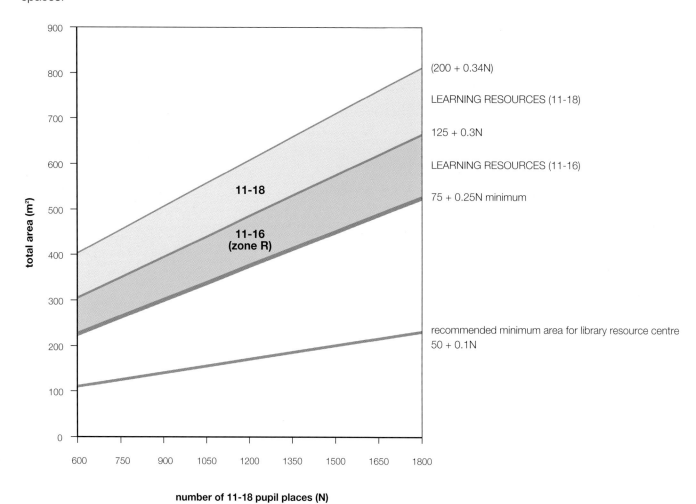

Learning Resource Areas

Learning resource areas are spaces used for learning but not timetabled for lessons. The total area (zones R and RR) for this category of space should include:

- the library resource centre[1] totalling at least 50m^2 plus 0.1m^2 for every pupil place (as in figure C.8);

- small group rooms throughout the school: at least one for every 150 pupil places, ideally spread around the school with some accessible directly from adjacent teaching spaces, to provide discrete, quiet spaces for learning support, for instance with a foreign language assistant, behaviour management or private counselling[2].

- SEN resource base for learning, behaviour, therapy support and case conferences;

- music group/practice rooms and an ensemble room totalling about four for each timetabled music room;

- specific area(s) for sixth form study where necessary.

And may also include:

- local resource areas within departments such as design and technology;

- a small recording studio or control room;

- a kiln room, darkroom or other ancillary areas;

- local ICT clusters (see ICT policy page 33).

The graph at figure C.8 (opposite) shows the total recommended area for all learning resources for an 11 to 16 school (zone R) and the area for a typical 11 to 18 school, based on zones R and RR.

Resources location policy

Learning resources accessible to pupils may all be in one library resource centre, or may also be found in local resource areas in some departments. There may be two libraries, for the main school and the sixth form for example.

Some facilities for the inclusion of pupils with SEN and disabilities may be central to the school, while others may be more dispersed through the school, to allow more immediate access for all and better integration.

Hint: avoid two-storey libraries, unless one floor can be unsupervised (for instance for sixth form study) while the librarian is on the other.

1. The library resource centre will include books, maps, CD-ROMs and artefacts available to the whole school. For more info see Cambridgeshire library service at http://www.camcnty.gov.uk/library.

2. Counselling can be useful for anti-bullying or personalised learning. See www.standards.dfes.gov.uk/personalisedlearning/.

Hint: do you need the darkroom? With the increasing popularity of digital photography, darkrooms for art may not be required. Dark conditions for physics or food testing may be best achieved through black-out blinds, to allow bigger groups and better utilisation.

Staff and Administration

The staff and administration area comprises most non-teaching areas (except storage and dining). The total staff and administration area (zones S and SS) must[1] include:

- an office for the head teacher, preferably of at least 12m²;

- medical inspection (MI) room, which, if there is a separate 'sick bay', may also be used for visiting therapists or other support for pupils with SEN and disabilities;

- work and social space for teaching staff, usually in the form of local departmental staff work rooms and a central staff room for social use (see policy below).

And should also include:

- offices for other senior teaching staff, particularly heads of year, who will need privacy for interviews and pastoral support;

- a main office with storage space for confidential records and a link to reception;

- additional accommodation for the bursar and other administrative staff;

- reprographic facilities[2].

It may also include:

- a meeting room or conference room[3] (usually adjacent to the head's office);

- caretaker's office;

- a 'sick bay', near to the reception and main office, where pupils who are sick can wait to be picked up (this is different to the MI room above).

Staff Location Policy

A social area for staff is usually centrally located. Staff work rooms may well be in a central staffroom, to encourage interaction, or in smaller department- or faculty-based workrooms (but not both, as the resultant space would be significantly underused).

1. The Education (School Premises) Regulations 1999 require any secondary school with over 120 pupils to have an office for the head teacher, and all schools to have an MI room and space for staff to work and socialise.

Hint: generous provision for individual offices will use up float with debatable effect! 8m² is recommended.

2. Reprographic facilities, and possibly ICT printing services, can usefully be positioned in a central room (but not in circulation areas) with appropriate staff and ventilation services available.

3. If there is not a meeting room, the head's office will usually need to be at least 30m² for meetings. A separate meeting room has the advantage that it can be used while the head's office is occupied.

Storage

The total area of storage (zones T and TT) must include:

- lockers or coat and bag storage for all pupils to store their personal belongings during the day, equivalent to at least 2m² per class group.

And should include the following teaching storage:

- shared accessible stores[1] for books and materials in general teaching subjects, one of at least 6m² for every general teaching department, preferably accessed from a circulation area or perhaps a shared staff workroom;

- specific accessible stores[1] for materials, equipment and pupils' work in progress in practical subjects: at least one of 6m² per teaching room except science laboratories, and two for each art room;

- large, central preparation/storage areas for science laboratories[2], food rooms and resistant materials workshops[3], ideally one for all science and one or two for design and technology;

- a shared instrument store of at least 10m² in music;

- PE equipment storage opening onto the long side of sports hall and activity studio: at least 10% of the size of the teaching space[4].

Some of this storage can be in teaching spaces[5]. However, this can reduce the usable area and flexibility of the room. Other storage should include:

- secure storage for valuable items such as examination papers and school and personal records;

- storage bays suitable for mobility equipment around the school, which may be used for temporary storage of bulk stock where there are no pupils with disabilities requiring such equipment[6];

- storage for maintenance equipment, cleaners' and caretaker's equipment;

- further separate storage for community use, for instance, of the sports hall.

Personal storage location policy: lockers and coat and bag racks may be located in classrooms, centrally (perhaps in a theatre style cloakroom, manned at certain times of the day), or in corridors or social areas: ideally in circulation areas of at least 2.7m wide[7], but not dead ends.

1. Accessible or 'walk-in' stores should be laid out, with an appropriate door, to allow items to be accessed from within the store room.

   Hint: storage in walk-in stores can be more economic on space and easier to manage than storage in teaching spaces.

2. Around 13m² per laboratory, see BB80: Science Accommodation in Secondary Schools: A Design Guide. TSO revised 2004. ISBN 0 11 271039 5.

3. A preparation room of at least 30m² for resistant materials and a smaller one for food. See BB81: Design and Technology Accommodation in Secondary Schools: A Design Guide. TSO revised 2004. ISBN 0 11 271039 5.

4. This is a minimum figure. Sport England recommend 12.5% and a minimum of 45m² for a one court hall. Note fire containment issues for mat storage.

5. Full height storage, such as lockers, coat and bag stores or cupboards, should be counted as storage area rather than teaching area.

6. Where pupils do need mobility aids, they may often have three items that need to be used at different times, with significant implications for storage space.

7. Building Regulations Approved Document M, 2004 requires corridors with lockers to be at least 2.7m wide.

Figure C.9: dining and social areas

Graph showing recommended areas for dining and social for 11 to 16 schools (zone U) and 11 to 18 schools with a typically sized sixth form (based on a proportional use of zone UU). Zone K indicates the recommended area for school kitchen facilities, including servery, staff and storage space (see page 47).

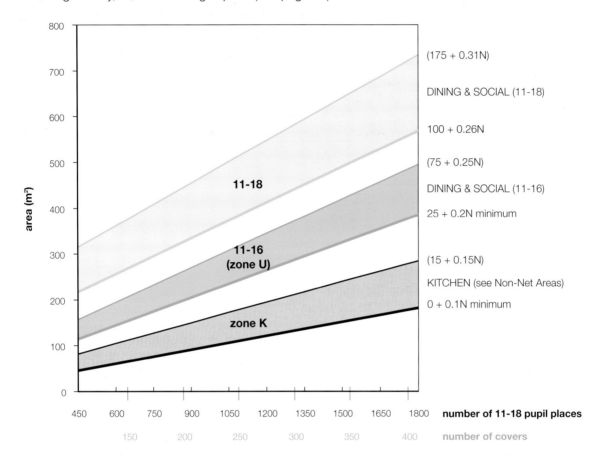

Dining and Social Areas

The total area of spaces used predominantly for dining and socialising (zones U and UU) should include:

- sufficient and appropriate areas for those pupils who wish to eat meals, based on a number of 'sittings';
- spaces specifically for sixth form pupils to use for social and non-teaching purposes.

And may include:

- further provision for cold meals or snacks, for instance from vending machines;
- social areas for other year or 'house' groups.

As well as a traditional dining hall, there are opportunities to create a much wider range of eating spaces, cafes, buffet areas or 'cyber-cafes' that offer nutritious food. Many schools use this facility to provide breakfast and other meals for both pupils and staff, and it can become a vibrant heart to the school community.

Figure C.9 (opposite) shows recommended dining and social area and kitchen areas. The area per 11 to 16 pupil is based on around 75% to 80% of pupils eating, and the equivalent of three sittings[1], plus time for gathering and dispersing. There is then an allowance of around 0.9m^2 per 'cover'.

The size of the kitchen facilities will also depend on the type of catering, but will generally be within zone K in figure C.9. School kitchens are covered under non-net spaces (page 47). Chair and table stores, which are needed if the space is to be used for other purposes, would be part of the storage category.

Dining location policy

Will the catering provision be available all day? If not, better use might be made of this space by providing the storage and resources to clear away chairs and tables for part of the day. As discussed on page 18, staggered lunch breaks can also reduce the demand for dining area. The implications of timetabling and alternative uses will have an impact on the design and location of the dining area.

1. The number of sittings, or the equivalent in a system of continuous throughput, will depend on the type of food served. Traditional hot meals average around 20 minutes per sitting, while 'fast food' options may average around 15 minutes.

Graph showing approximate recommended standards for
non-net areas, assuming no supplementary net area. Zones
without a an identifying letter are based on a percentage of the
recommended net area, as on page 45. For kitchens see zone K
in figure C.9 on page 42.

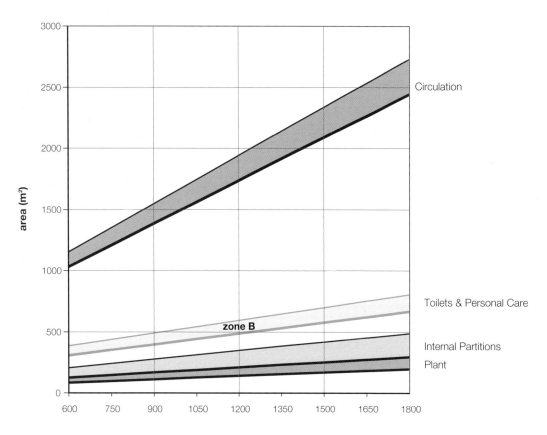

Non-Net Area of Buildings

The non-net area is made up of variable areas that are not included in the net area of the school. It comprises the five categories of space listed below, plus non-net areas supporting any supplementary net areas for non-school or support functions (see page 49).

- toilets and personal care   (zones S and SS);
- kitchen facilities   (zone K, page 42);
- circulation   (25% to 30% of net);
- plant, such as boilers   (2% to 3% of net);
- the area of internal walls   (3% to 6% of net).

The first two categories of space will depend on the number of pupils, community use and, for kitchens, the type of catering arrangements in the school. The last three categories will generally be directly proportional to the net area, so it is important to include any supplementary net area in the total net area before calculating the requirement for these areas.

The bottom of the zone, or the lower of the proportions of net shown in brackets, represents the minimum recommended area for that category of space.

The total area for each of these categories should be at least the minimum recommended in this bulletin. If any of the individual categories are insufficient for the site[1] (even if the total non-net area is enough) it is likely to compromise the best use of the buildings.

An area greater than the minimum but within the zone or range above will usually be required for each category. The overall recommended gross area of about 142.5% of the total net area (such that net area is about 70% of gross) allows for the area of each category of space to average around the middle of each zone.

1. **Split sites** (where a significant part of the school is provided on each site) may need to use the full formulae for toilets and personal care or kitchens for each site that requires changing rooms or kitchen facilities.

Toilets and Personal Care

The total area of toilet and personal care facilities (zones S and SS on pages 26 and 28) must[1] include:

- toilets for pupils: at least one for every 20 pupils;

- separate toilets for staff: usually at least one for every ten full-time equivalent members of staff[2] (not including catering staff);

- accessible toilets for disabled pupils, staff or visitors[3];

- changing rooms with showers, near to indoor and outdoor sports provision.

And should also include:

- changing facilities for staff;

- a specialist hygiene room containing a shower, sluice, toilet, a changing trolley, fixed or mobile hoist and space for assistants[4].

Some of the spaces listed above may be designed to allow facilities appropriate to:

- adult community use, usually outside the school day[5];

- particular religious requirements, including orientation and ablutions.

The location and design of toilet and changing room facilities should balance the demands for both privacy and adequate supervision.

Normally it is sufficient to provide changing facilities for half a year group with equal and separate facilities for boys and girls in co-educational schools and further changing rooms for the sixth form[6]. Showers should generally be in the form of separate cubicles, with approximately one for every six or seven pupils changing[7]. In addition, at least one accessible changing area (with a sanitary fitting, wash basin and shower) should be provided in each changing area.

Toilet location policy: the size, location and design of toilets can have an impact on the potential for bullying, supervision and inclusion: from one or two central toilet 'blocks' to smaller facilities in every department, perhaps with fully accessible cubicles in each toilet.

1. The Education (School Premises) Regulations 1999 require one toilet for every 20 pupils, (rounded up to the next whole number) and changing facilities with showers for all pupils of 11 years or over.

2. Appropriate provision for staff is suggested in the Workplace (Health, Safety and Welfare) Regulations 1992, Approved Code of Practice.

3. Refer to Building Regulations, Approved Document M and BS 8300.

4. See The Manual Handling Operations Regulations 1992 as amended 2002 and draft Health and Safety Matters for SEN: Moving and Handling Pupils/Students HSE.

5. For information on changing facilities for community use see Sport England guidance note 'Sports Halls: Design' (ISBN 1 86078 094 6).

6. At least an area of 0.9m² per pupil plus 5m² for disabled users should be provided.

7. An area of at least 1.25m² per cubicle will allow a separate dry-off area.

Kitchen Facilities

The kitchen area (zone K on page 42) is often approximately half the area of the dining facilities, depending on the type of catering. It must[1] include:

- facilities for preparing food and drink, and washing up afterwards, where it is needed.

It should also include:

- food store rooms;
- facilities for catering staff, including changing areas, toilets and a chef's office;
- space for serving the food.

The size of the core preparation area will depend on the equipment needed, which in turn will depend on the type of preparation system to be used: from traditional, through cook-chill to pre-prepared 'fast food'. There should be easy access for deliveries and a secure site for bins.

Circulation

An area at least equivalent to 25% of the total net area (including supplementary net area) will be required to ensure that:

- all rooms are accessed from a circulation route, except store rooms accessed directly from learning spaces[2]:
- corridors leading to more than one or two teaching rooms have a clear width of at least 1.8m (1.9m in new schools and 2.7m where there are lockers)[3];
- smaller corridors have a clear width of at least 1.2m.

Plant

An area equivalent to at least 2% of the total net area will be needed to accommodate boiler rooms and a server room. Further area will generally be needed if ventilation plant, chimneys or vertical ducts are included in the design.

Internal Walls

The area of internal walls[4] will occupy an area equivalent to at least 3% of the net area, and up to 6% if the walls are wider to allow for acoustic separation and/or to provide thermal mass.

Hint: Effective and creative use can be made of circulation area: from spaces for informal gathering and display of work off corridors to large atria. However, ensure that any extra space can be effectively used if it is to be heated, lit and maintained.

2. Circulation area can be the routes within a larger room or atrium, and the remaining area will count towards the usable net area of the school if it is wider than 1.2m. See 'Assessing the Net Capacity of Schools' DfES/0739/2001 at www.dfes.gov.uk/netcapacity.

3. For details of access requirements in circulation areas refer to Building Regulations Approved Document M, 2004 and BS 8300.

4. The area of internal walls is included in the measured internal gross area of the buildings.

Part C: The Buildings

47

Figure C.11: Examples of Supplementary Net Areas

The table below gives examples of facilities or provision that would normally require supplementary net area, and a proportional amount of non-net area of circulation, plant and internal walls. These are listed under headings that match those used to identify area that is measured but excluded in net capacity assessments.

provision	likely funding
Early Years and Childcare	
• crèche	LEA
• child-care provision out of school hours other than support spaces for use of normal school facilities.	LEA/Sure Start
Adult Learning and Skills	
• adult Learning and Skills Facilities not available to the school during the school day;	Learning and Skills Council (LSC);
• centres for LEA Services, such as staff training;	LEA
• City Learning Centres	LEA
Specially Resourced Provision	
• Additional facilities providing a number of places for pupils with a specific range of SEN or disabilities (such as a support centre for 26 pupils with sensory impairments);	LEA/BSF
• Additional facilities providing a number of places for pupils with behaviour management problems, such as Learning Support Units	LEA/BSF
• Pupil Referral Units	LEA/BSF
• Accommodation for LEA designated support services, including peripatetic support staff	LEA
Extended Schools and Other	
• extra facilities to allow community use during the school day or not available to the school (such as a club room or bar)	Local Authority (LA) leisure or local community groups
• health care or 'multi-agency' provision other than joint use of MI or physiotherapy room or other facilities intended primarily for pupil use	Primary Care Trust
• public library	LA library services or DCMS
• indoor swimming pool	LA leisure services, DCMS or Lottery Fund
• chapel or prayer room (if it is not available to the school for normal teaching)	Voluntary aided governors liability or diocese

Supplementary Areas

The briefing team should assess if there is a need for any supplementary net area within the project[1]. It is important to note that a dedicated, additional funding stream needs to be identified for any supplementary net area (unless it already exists in appropriate accommodation), as discussed in relation to extended schools provision on page 19.

There are three types of spaces that fall within this category:

* *area to accommodate the enhancement of school facilities:* this will include spaces which have been enlarged beyond the recommended 'standard', for instance to allow for spectators in the sports hall;

* *area to accommodate extra support facilities:* this will include separate spaces available to the school for specific uses, such as SEN specialist resources, City Learning Centres or Learning Support Units;

* *non-school provision:* this is separate space not normally available to the school, for example facilities for adult education or community use during the day.

Figure C.11 (opposite) lists some of the most likely types of non-school or support facilities[2] that would need supplementary area, and the possible funding sources that would cover this.

Supplementary area would not normally be required to accommodate small extended schools provision such as a parents'/ community room or office, or the priorities of general inclusion, specialist schools or vocational teaching.

Although this bulletin does not include recommended standards for the supplementary net area, it is very important to include the desired allowance for supplementary net area in the total net area and the accommodation schedule. This will ensure that the allowance for non-net area is sufficient to allow for the circulation, plant and internal walls related to the supplementary area.

1. Non-school and support functions require further area over and above the recommended net area. They are not expected to be included in the float.

Hint: When considering the brief for a complete overhaul of the school, ensure the needs of all stakeholders are included, to avoid any current temporary provision having to remain for the want of funding.

2. As defined in Assessing the Net Capacity of Schools DfES/0739/2001 **www.dfes.gov.uk/ netcapacity**.

Figure D.1: gross site area and net site area defined

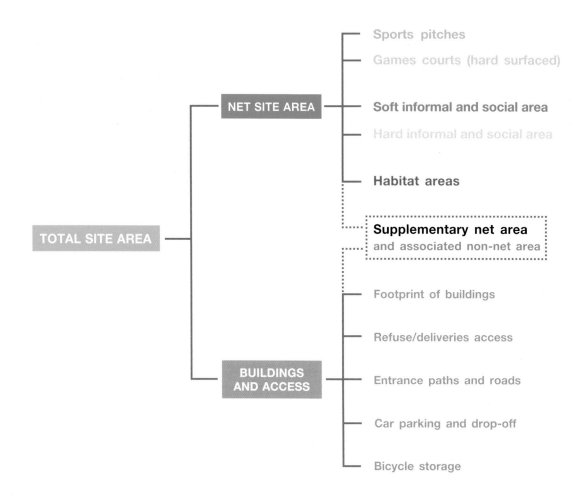

Part D:
The Site

This part deals with the site area for a school. School grounds are a valuable resource and have a significant effect on the ethos of the school and the quality of education pupils receive[1].

Total Site Area

The total, or gross, area of the site can be separated into two categories:

- *net site area*, legally the 'playing field' area, which can be accurately calculated from the formulae in appendix 1 and in figure D.2; plus any agreed supplementary net site area; and

- *buildings and access area*, which will be more variable depending on the configuration of new and existing buildings and site constraints, but will generally increase in proportion to the net site area.

The total of these categories gives the total (gross) area of the site, as described in figure D.1 opposite.

The total site area required will depend on the design of the site and the layout of the buildings. Generally, the total site area needed for a new secondary school may vary between 110% and 125% of the net site area (such that the net site area is 80% to 90% of the total), depending on the layout and type of site[2].

The total net site area required by an inclusive community school should not normally need to exceed the recommended net site area for the number of pupil places and age range of the school.

Further supplementary net site area, and a proportional increase in buildings and access area, may be needed if there are specially resourced non-school or support functions on the school site (as discussed on page 58).

Figure D.3 on page 54 shows a typical site plan with the various categories of net site area and buildings and access area shown.

1. Building Bulletin 71: The Outdoor Classroom second edition, TSO 1999 (ISBN 0-11-271061-1) and Building Bulletin 85: School Grounds, A Guide to Good Practice, TSO 1997 (ISBN 0-11-270990-7), give advice on the educational design and management of external spaces.

Hint: Site layout: dispersing buildings on the site may be easier for community access, and gives identity to departments or age related bases, such as a sixth form, and perhaps better supervision of enclosed outdoor areas. Linked, concentrated buildings can offer circulation without going outside, and more adaptability.

2. This calculation only relates to the total area of the site including playing fields. The proportion of buildings and access area on a confined site, or one where playing fields are elsewhere, will be much higher.

Figures D.2: site area

Graph showing recommended standards for total and net site area and for sports pitches for any secondary school, and the statutory minimum 'team game playing field' area required by the Education (School Premises) Regulations 1999.

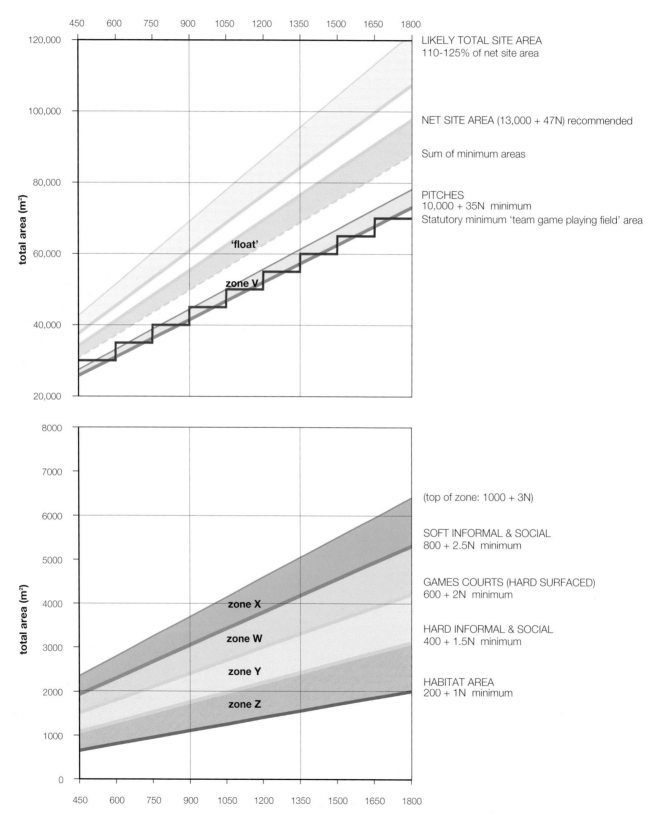

LIKELY TOTAL SITE AREA
110-125% of net site area

NET SITE AREA (13,000 + 47N) recommended

Sum of minimum areas

PITCHES
10,000 + 35N minimum
Statutory minimum 'team game playing field' area

'float'

zone V

(top of zone: 1000 + 3N)

SOFT INFORMAL & SOCIAL
800 + 2.5N minimum

GAMES COURTS (HARD SURFACED)
600 + 2N minimum

HARD INFORMAL & SOCIAL
400 + 1.5N minimum

HABITAT AREA
200 + 1N minimum

zone X

zone W

zone Y

zone Z

number of pupil places (any age) (N)

Defining the total site area is an important step for a new school. Reviewing the site area against the graph of recommended areas (figure D.2, opposite) is also useful when considering alterations to an existing school. The range in the graph allows for variation in the shape and contours of the site, and size of the building complex.

Net Site Area: Playing Fields

The net site area, known as the 'playing fields area' in some cases[1], is the total of the following five categories of space:

- sports pitches   (zone V);
- games courts (hard surfaced)   (zone W);
- soft informal and social   (zone X);
- hard informal and social   (zone Y);
- habitat areas   (zone Z);

plus any supplementary net site area needed for non-school or support functions.

The bottom of each zone, which can be calculated using the formulae shown, represents the minimum recommended area for that category of space.

The total area for each of these categories should generally be at least the minimum recommended in this bulletin (i.e. the bottom of the zone)[2].

An area greater than the minimum but within the zone will usually be designed for each category. The overall recommended net and gross area allows for the area of each category of space to average around the middle of each zone, through the provision of some 'float'[3], as with the buildings area.

In confined sites, the sports pitches area may be provided on a nearby site and/or through a single all-weather pitch[4]. Where there are no other outdoor PE facilities on the site, a multi-use games area (see page 55) within zone W should be provided on the site, to allow easy access for outdoor team games. The area of the remaining three categories of space may only be achievable at the zone or area below that recommended for normal sites.

The informal and social areas and Habitat can also be a rich resource for teaching work related to vocational courses such as horticulture, gardening, landscape design, art and design and land management.

1. Section 77(7) of the School Standards and Framework Act 1998, which is designed to protect school playing fields, defines 'playing fields' as 'any land in the open air which is provided for the purposes of physical education or recreation, other than any prescribed description of land'.

2. In **split sites** the total area for each category across all sites should be used. So, for instance, the sports pitches may all be provided on one site.

3. **What is the float?** When you add together the recommended minimum area of each category of space, the total will be around 5 to 10% less than the recommended standard for the total net site area. This difference provides the 'float' which can be used to enhance some areas, depending on the design of the site.

4. All-weather pitches count twice in area calculations. See page 55.

Figure D.3: typical site plan

A site plan of the secondary school used in the case study on pages 12 to 14, showing the different categories of site area

pages 12 to 14

Key:
1 Pitches (49,013m²)
2 Games courts (2,875m²)
3 Soft informal and social (5,275m²)
4 Hard informal and social (3,666m²)
5 Habitat (3,023m²)

Remaining area is 'Buildings and Access Area'

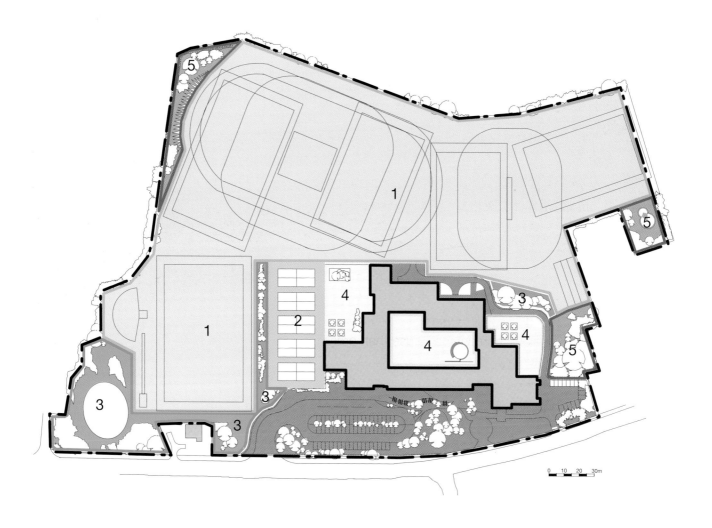

0 10 20 30m

Outdoor PE Facilities

The first two categories of net site area add up to the area used for Physical Education (PE) and will generally match the statutory requirement[1] for 'team game playing field area'.

Careful attention should be given to the layout of pitches, courts and practice areas[2]. Their location, size and shape should be based on a number of considerations including the statutory requirements, safety considerations, gradient, relationships between winter games pitches and summer athletics and cricket provision, orientation of pitches and accessibility[3].

Sports Pitches

The total area of sports pitches (zone V) must include playing field area laid out to suit team games including:

- winter pitches for the school's preferred team games, such as football, rugby and hockey;

- overlapping summer pitches, such as cricket[4], a 400m athletics track and facilities for field events.

All-weather pitches, including synthetic turf pitches[5] or polymeric surfaces[6], allow more intensive use than grass and, particularly with floodlighting, can also offer a popular community resource.

The area of all-weather pitches can be counted twice for the purposes of both these guidelines and regulations, as they can be used for significantly more than the seven hours a week required of team game playing fields.

Games Courts

In new schools, the total area of hard surfaced games courts (zone W in figure D.2) should include:

- a multi-use games area[7], with three netball courts overlaid, with critical dimensions of 60m x 33m plus margins;

- further tennis/netball courts in larger schools.

Laying out a variety of courts within a single multi-use games area makes supervision easier and extends the range of games.

In existing schools, a similar amount of hard surfaced area should be laid out for games[8].

1. The Education (School Premises) Regulations 1999 define 'team game playing fields' as 'playing fields which, having regard to their configuration, are suitable for the playing of team games and which are laid out for that purpose'.

2. Refer to Sport England 'Handbook of Sports and Recreational Building Design Volume 1: Outdoor Sports'.

3. Refer to Building Bulletin 91: Access for Disabled People to School Buildings, TSO 1999 (ISBN 0-11-271062-X), Building Bulletin 94: Inclusive School Design, TSO 2001 (ISBN 0-11-271109-X) and Sport England Guidance Note Access for Disabled People (ISBN 1 86078 149 7).

4. Cricket squares are often fenced in winter to protect the surface, as long as there is space to accommodate winter pitches around them.

5. See Sport England Guidance Note no. 596: 'Synthetic Turf Pitches'.

6. Such as shredded rubber bonded with bitumen, latex or polyurethane, on a base of concrete laid to fall. See Sport England Guidance Notes and BS7044 Part 4: 'Artificial Sports Surfaces – Specification for Surfaces for Multi-Sport Use'.

7. See Sport England Guidance Note 374: 'Multi-Use Games Areas'.

8. This area will count towards the current Education (School Premises) Regulations 1999 requirement for team game playing fields only if it is used for team games.

Informal and Social Areas

A variety of informal and social areas should be created to suit the learning development and cultural needs of pupils during breaks and before and after school, and for a range of more formal curriculum needs. These will include soft-surfaced, usually grassed, areas and hard-surfaced courtyards, paths and playgrounds.

Increasingly, the landscape design of these areas is being given equal status to the building design. It also has a great potential for promoting a sense of ownership of space by pupils and staff, thereby encouraging people to take greater care of their surroundings.

Soft-surfaced Areas

The 'soft' areas should be conveniently situated, safe and provide some shade. Imaginative landscaping and planting can provide a range of outdoor areas, including quiet areas that may be particularly appropriate to pupils with SEN or disabilities.

The total area (zone X in figure D.2) could include:

- grassed space to sit and socialise;

- sloping grass areas for spectators or a natural amphitheatre;

- landscaped or planted areas near to buildings.

Hard-surfaced Areas

To complement the soft informal and social areas, there should be hard-surfaced playgrounds and sheltered space for socialising and for the encouragement of healthy, active, creative outdoor play. Appropriate site furniture, such as seating, to accommodate larger outdoor study groups and smaller more intimate areas, is important. This area should also provide scope, through a range of hard surfaces and structures, for pupils to engage in outdoor art, theatre, dance and design.

The total area (zone Y in figure D.2) should include:

- hard-surfaced, sheltered space to sit and socialise, including those accessed from adjacent teaching spaces;

- large hard-surfaced areas for more active play.

And may also include rooftop play areas or 'playdecks' at upper floors that may be available to pupils in confined sites.

© Learning Through Landscapes

Habitat areas

Habitat areas can include a range of outdoor classroom spaces and designs to provide a valuable resource for teaching and learning across the whole curriculum, as well as for children's emotional, social and cultural development[1]. They are important for involving pupils in the life and management of the school.

The total habitat area (zone Z) should include grounds developed for a range of supervised activities, for instance meadowland, wildlife habitats (such as ponds), gardens and outdoor science areas to support the curriculum.

1. Details and examples are available from Learning Through Landscapes at **www.ltl.org.uk** and include a range of advisory services on the use, design and management of school grounds.

Buildings and Access Area

The non-net site area will vary depending on the configuration of the site and buildings. It will include:

- the 'footprint' of all buildings;

- delivery access;

- refuse areas (secure or distant from the buildings);

And will usually include:

- entrance paths, roads and related landscaping not normally available to pupils;

- car parking (usually equivalent to one parking bay per teacher plus a few bays for visitors and the disabled).

And may include:

- space for coaches, buses or taxis to safely drop-off pupils, particularly those with SEN or disabilities;

- secure bicycle storage for pupils.

It is most important to consider means of separating children's pedestrian access from vehicular circulation, delivery areas and parking and for providing adequate, visible secure bicycle storage for older pupils.

Supplementary Site Area

As discussed on page 49, any school may have supplementary areas for non-school or support functions. Any site area associated with these functions will be a supplementary site area, and may also need to be funded through other joined-up funding streams.

Some examples are play space for a crèche, extra car parking for community use, or enhancements to sports provision also used by the community.

Appendices

The following pages include two sets of example schedules of accommodation and the key formulae for all secondary schools[1].

Appendix 1 shows a full schedule of accommodation for four typical sizes of 11 to 16 secondary school and two typical sizes of sixth form. Each is shown only as an example, and is not intended as more than a guide to the possible options.

To highlight the various options available, Appendix 2 shows a variety of schedules for one size of school and, separately, its sixth form.

In practice, 11 to 18 schools would have the opportunity to be more flexible within the overall area recommended for each category of space, rather than treating the 11 to 16 and sixth form cohorts separately.

Figures highlighted in red in Appendix 1 indicate areas that are within the 'float' and could be used for other purposes. For instance, the extra area used to enhance the size of the classrooms to 60m^2 could be used for separate ICT rooms or clusters. The area of the activity studio could be used for other purposes depending on the preferences of the school[2].

Appendix 2 shows possible options in more detail, and lists them under subject headings. It takes a single size of 11 to 16 school, at 900 pupil places, and a typical sixth form for the same school, and shows different schedules for both. These options are used to highlight a number of likely variations that any school may choose.

- The configuration of classrooms is explored in the first few rows, under the subjects of English, modern foreign languages, humanities and mathematics[3]: option A uses some large classrooms, which might have ICT at the back or available as laptops or tablets, and some at the minimum recommended size; options B and C use ICT clusters within departments and option D assumes all classrooms to be 60m^2.

- The number of timetabled rooms varies in each option, in line with variations in the curriculum depending on the emphasis preferred by the school (for instance, because of a specialism). For instance, in the 11 to 16 schedules,

2. In each case, the rooms have been chosen because their area most closely matches the amount of float used in the category of space in this example. The choice of room does not necessarily indicate that the type of room is optional – this will depend on the priorities and curriculum of the school.

3. Each option is achieved within an area equivalent to the number of classrooms at 60m^2 each.

the number of classrooms can vary from 20 to 23, the number of science laboratories from 6 to 8 and the number of design and technology rooms from 4 to 6 (seven including an untimetabled design resource area).

- All the 11 to 16 schedules include a four-court sports hall, but the activity hall or gymnasium may not be required or may be larger to provide a one-court hall suitable for community use, for instance in a sports college.

- The sixth form in option X uses standard classrooms and a small sixth from study area in each department, while option Y uses seminar rooms and a single sixth form study area typical of schools that choose to have a [separate] sixth form centre.

Any two or three departments may be linked as a faculty and other variations are obviously possible, including 'house' structures and 'schools within schools'[1].

The colours of the text in Appendix 2 match those used in figures C.1 and C.2 to identify the six categories of net area and, in black, the non-net areas.

It is worth noting that the total area of each of the six categories of net area are within the recommended areas given in the relevant zones on pages 26 and 28.

Appendix 3 sets out the key formulae for calculating the minimum recommended area of the six categories of net area, the total net area (including 'float') and the likely gross area of both buildings and sites. Together, these can be used to calculate the requirements for any secondary school, including middle deemed secondary and 16 to 19 schools.

The area per pupil place for sixth forms in schools is different to that used by the Learning and Skills Council[2] for sixth form colleges by a proportion equivalent to the number of hours that students are expected to be taught. In sixth form colleges, this may be from 15 to 20 hours an week, whereas in a school it would be expected to be from 20 to 25 hours a week (with a proportional increase in area required).

1. As discussed in various exemplar designs. See www.teachernet.gov.uk/exemplars.

2. See Learning and Skills Council Circular 02/20 'Guidance on College Property Strategies' at www.lsc.gov.uk/National/Documents/Series/Circulars.

Appendix 1

Example Schedules for various sizes of schools

	max. group size	average area (m²)	net capacity places	11 to 16 600 642 to 577		900 850 to 945		1200 1125 to 1251		1500 1399 to 1555		sixth form 100		250	
TEACHING															
basic teaching															
general teaching															
seminar room	16	43	26									2	86	5	215
classroom (see figure C.5)	30	56	30	14	784	21	1176	28	1568	34	1904	2	112	2	112
further classroom area	–	4	–	14	56	21	84	28	112	34	136	2	8	2	8
IT/business studies room	20	60	20									3	180	6	360
IT room	30	77	27	1	77	2	154	3	231	4	308				
science laboratory	30	90	30	5	450	7	630	9	810	11	990	1	90	2	180
design and technology				4		6		8		10					
food room	20	101	24	1	101	1	101	2	202	2	202				
resistant materials (incl. heat bay or CADCAM)	20	112	27	1	112	2	224	2	224	3	336				
electronics and control systems	20	90	30	1	90	1	90	2	180	2	180				
constructional textiles	20	90	30	1	90	1	90	1	90	2	180				
graphics room	20	77	27			1	77	1	77	1	77				
art				1		2		3		4					
large art room (textiles or 3D)	30	105	30	1	105	2	210	2	210	2	210				
general art room	30	90	30					1	90	2	180			1	90
music				1		2		2		3					
music recital	30	90	28	1	90	1	90	1	90	1	90				
music classroom	30	67	23			1	67	1	67	2	134			1	67
drama studio	30	90	28					1	90	1	90				
audio visual studio	30	90	28							1	90				
halls				3		3		3		3					
4-court sports hall	60	594	60	1	594	1	594	1	594	1	594				
activity studio	30	150	30	1	150	1	150	1	180	1	180				
main hall	2-5 year groups	–	30	1	200	1	280	1	290	1	300	add	30	add	75
total timetabled spaces				29		43		57		71		8		17	
learning resource areas															
SEN resource base	8	20	–	1	20	1	20	1	20	1	20				
small group room (SEN etc)	6	16	–	1	16	1	16	2	32	2	32				
small group/interview room (foreign language assistant etc)	4	10	–	2	20	3	30	4	40	5	50	1	10	1	10
music group/practice rooms	6	7	–	4	28	7	49	7	49	10	70	3	21		
music ensemble room	10	20	–	1	20	1	20	1	20	2	40				
recording/ control room	4	12	–	1	12	1	12	1	12	1	12				
kiln room	–	4	–	1	4	1	4	1	4	1	4				
darkroom	5	12	–	1	12	1	12	1	12	1	12				
library resource centre and careers	N/10	–	30	1	124	1	155	1	186	1	217	add	10	add	24
sixth form study areas												1	60	1	90
art/ design resource area	20	43	–									1	43	1	43
Total Teaching Area				3155		4355		5480		6638		629		1295	

	max. group size	average area (m²)	net capacity places	11 to 16 600		900		1200		1500		sixth form 100		250	
Staff and administration															
head's office	–	12	–	1	12	1	12	1	12	1	12				
meeting room	–	–	–	1	16	1	16	1	20	1	24				
offices (senior management, head of year, SENco, librarian, caretaker, etc.)	–	8	–	10	80	13	104	15	120	18	144	1	8	1	8
community and other offices	–	8	–	4	32	3	24	3	24	2	16			1	8
SEN therapy/MI room	8	18	–	1	18	1	18	1	18	1	18				
entrance/reception and adjacent sick bay	–	–	–	1	13	1	16	1	19	1	22				
general office	–	–	–	1	33	1	48	1	63	1	78			add	8
staff room (social)	–	–	–	1	50	1	60	1	70	1	80	add	10	add	24
staff work rooms	–	–	–	5	70	5	100	5	130	5	160	1	20	1	43
reprographics	–	–	–	1	20	1	26	1	32	1	38				
ICT technician	–	8	–	1	8	1	8	1	8	1	8				
Storage (teaching)															
walk-in teaching stores:															
general teaching/IT/library	–	3	–	6	18	9	27	11	33	14	42	4	12	8	24
off practical, music or drama spaces	–	6	–	7	42	13	78	18	108	25	150			3	18
instrument and external stores	–	10	–	2	20	2	20	2	20	2	20				
PE stores	–	72+15	–	2	87	2	87	2	87	2	87				
science preparation room(s) and chemical store	–	13 per lab	–		65		91		117		143	add	23	add	36
food preparation room	–	12	–	1	12	1	12	1	12	1	12				
resistant materials prep. room	–	50	–	1	50	1	50	1	50	1	50				
Storage (non-teaching)															
central stock	–	–	–		12		15		18		24	add	4	add	6
SENco/wheelchair/appliances	–	12	–		12		12		12		12				
secure/exam/community stores	–	8	–	2	16	2	16	2	16	2	16	1	8	1	8
lockers for personal storage	–	–	–		42		63		84		105		9		23
community lockers (out of school hours)	–	4	–		4		4		4		4				
chair store	–	–	–	1	12	1	18	1	24	1	30	add	3	add	8
maintenance store	–	8	–	1	8	1	8	2	16	2	16	add	4	add	4
cleaners' stores	–	1.5	–	4	6	6	9	8	12	10	15	2	3	2	3
Dining/social areas															
dining area (hot meals)	N/4	–	–		160		215		270		325		36		80
social and sandwich areas	–	–	–		30		35		40		45		7		10
sixth form social	–	–	–										90		120
Total Net Area					**4103**		**5527**		**6919**		**8334**		**866**		**1726**
(BB98 recommendation)					(4120)		(5530)		(6940)		(8350)		(870)		(1725)
catering facilities	–	–	–												
kitchen (incl staff and stores)	–	–	–	1	68	1	101	1	134	1	167	1	11	1	28
toilets (and personal care)															
pupil changing rooms and showers	N/10	–	–	2	100	2	134	2	168	2	202	add	34	add	54
hygiene facilities	–	30	–		30		30		30		30		6		12
pupil toilets	–	2.6	–	varies	90	varies	129	varies	168	varies	207	varies	14	varies	34
staff toilets	–	3.5	–	varies	21	varies	32	varies	42	varies	53	varies	4	varies	11
circulation — assuming net around 70% of gross					1128		1520		1903		2292		238		475
plant — including server					118		153		188		223		25		46
partitions					187		247		306		365		36		72
Total Net Area					**5845**		**7873**		**9858**		**11783**		**1233**		**2457**
net as percentage of gross					70.2%		70.2%		70.2%		70.2%		70.2%		70.2%

Appendix 2

Example Schedules of Various Curricula

basic teaching
  halls
    learning resources
      staff and administration
        storage
          dining and social
            non-net

				900 11 to 16 Places								215 16 to 18 Places			
curriculum emphasis				option A: science, design and technology		option B: music, sport		option C: performing arts, business and enterprise		option D: languages, art, humanities, mathematics and ICT		option X: science, design and technology, music, performing arts		option Y: languages, art, humanities, maths & ICT, business, sport	
net capacity range				834 to 927		850 to 945		865 to 962		882 to 981		137 to 361		153 to 378	
	max. group size	average area (m²)	net capacity places	number of rooms	total area	number of rooms	total area	number of rooms	total area	number of rooms	total area	number of rooms	total area	number of rooms	total area
English, Modern Foreign Languages, Humanities and Mathematics		60		20	1200	21	1260	22	1320	23	1380	4	220	7	385
seminar rooms (sixth form)	16	43	26	–	–	–	–	–	–	–	–	–	–	4	172
large classrooms	30	66	30	8	528	4	264	–	–	–	–	–	–	–	–
min. classrooms	30	56	30	12	672	12	672	22	1232	–	–	–	–	–	–
classrooms	30	60	30	–	–	5	300	–	–	23	1380	4	240	3	180
ICT clusters	10	varies	–	–	–	1	24	4	88	–	–	–	–	1	32
small group rooms (including FLA) or sixth form study	12	varies	–	3	30	3	30	3	30	3	30	1	30	1	10
Head of Year offices	–	8	–	4	32	4	32	4	32	4	32	–	–	–	–
staff workrooms	–	20	–	2	40	2	40	2	40	2	40	add	14	add	21
general teaching store rooms	–	3	–	7	21	7	21	7	21	8	24	2	6	3	9
Information Technology/ Business Studies				2		2		3		4		4		7	
IT/BS rooms (sixth form or KS4)	20	60	20	–	–	–	–	1	60	1	60	3	180	5	300
IT room or language lab.	30	77	27	2	154	2	154	2	154	3	231	1	77	2	154
ICT technician	–	8	–	1	8	1	8	1	8	2	16	–	–	–	–
Head of Year office	–	8	–	1	8	1	8	1	8	1	8	–	–	–	–
staff workroom (shared with science)	–	20	–	1	20	1	20	1	20	1	20	add	7	add	14
ICT store room	–	3	–	1	3	1	3	1	3	1	3	1	3	2	6
server	–	8	–	1	8	1	8	1	8	1	8	–	–	–	–
Science				8		7		7		6		3		2	
science laboratories	30	90	30	8	720	7	630	7	630	6	540	3	270	2	180
small group room or sixth form study (shared with IT/BS)	–	30	–	–	–	–	–	–	–	–	–	1	30	–	–
science preparation room(s) and chemicals store	–	varies	–		104		91		91		78	add	49	add	36
Design and Technology				6 plus resource		6		5		4		1		0	
food room	20	101	24	1	101	1	101	1	101	1	101	–	–	–	–
food preparation room	–	12	–	1	12	1	12	1	12	1	12	–	–	–	–
resistant materials	20	varies	27	2	224	2	224	2	224	1	116	–	–	–	–
resistant materials prep room	–	50	–	1	50	1	50	1	50	1	50	–	–	–	–
electronics and control systems	20	90	30	1	90	1	90	1	90	1	90	–	–	–	–
textiles	20	77	27	1	77	1	77	1	77	1	77	–	–	–	–
graphic products	20	90	30	1	90	1	90	–	–	–	–	1	90	–	–
design resource area	12	50	16	1	50	–	–	–	–	–	–	–	–	–	–
staff work room (shared with art)	–	20	–	1	20	1	20	1	20	1	20	add	7	–	–
practical store rooms	–	6	–	7	42	7	42	5	30	5	30	1	6	–	–
Art				2		2		2		3		0		1	
large art room (textiles or 3D)	30	105	30	2	210	2	210	2	210	2	210	–	–	–	–
kiln room	–	4	–	1	4	1	4	1	4	1	4	–	–	–	–
general art room	30	90	30	–	–	–	–	–	–	1	90	–	–	1	90
darkroom	5	12	–	1	12	–	–	1	12	1	12	–	–	–	–
art/design resource area	20	varies	–	–	–	–	–	–	–	1	43	1	30	–	–
practical store rooms	–	6	–	4	24	4	24	4	24	6	36	0	0	2	12
Music and Drama				1		2		3		3		1		0	
music recital	30	90	28	1	90	1	90	1	90	1	90	–	–	–	–
music classroom	30	67	23	–	–	1	67	–	–	1	67	1	67	–	–
music group/practice rooms	6	7	–	4	28	7	49	4	28	7	49	3	21	–	–
music ensemble room	10	20	–	1	20	1	20	1	20	1	20	1	30	–	–
recording/ control room	4	12	–	1	12	1	12	1	12	1	12	–	–	–	–
staff work room (shared with PE)	–	20	–	1	20	1	20	1	20	1	20	add	7	–	–
Drama studio	30	90	28	0	0	0	0	1	90	1	90	–	–	–	–
Audio-visual studio (media studies)	30	90	28	0	0	0	0	1	90	–	–	–	–	–	–
instrument store	–	10	–	1	10	1	10	1	10	1	10	–	–	–	–
music and drama stores	–	6	–	1	6	2	12	3	18	1	6	1	6	–	–

basic teaching
　halls
　　learning resources
　　　staff and administration
　　　　storage
　　　　　dining and social
　　　　　　non-net

	max. group size	average area (m²)	net capacity places	900 11 to 16 Places option A: science, design and technology — no. of rooms	total area	option B: music, sport — no. of rooms	total area	option C: performing arts, business and enterprise — no. of rooms	total area	option D: languages, art, humanities, mathematics and ICT — no. of rooms	total area	215 16 to 18 Places option X: science, design and technology, music, performing arts — no. of rooms	total area	option Y: languages, art, humanities, maths & ICT, business, sport — no. of rooms	total area
Physical Education															
4-court sports hall	60	594	60	1	594	1	594	1	594	1	594	–	–	–	–
activity studio	30	150	30	1	150	1	180	–	–	–	–	–	–	–	–
multi-gym	12	40	–	–	–	1	40	–	–	–	–	–	–	–	–
PE and external stores	–	varies	–	2	97	3	115	1	80	1	80	–	–	–	–
pupil changing rooms and showers	N/10	59		2	118	2	118	2	118	2	118	add	40	add	40
staff and visitor changing rooms and showers		8		2	16	3	24	2	16	2	16	–	–	–	–
Central Resources															
main hall	–	varies	30	1	280	1	280	1	310	1	280	add	65	add	65
library resource centre and careers	N/10	varies	30	1	155	1	140	1	155	1	155	add	20	add	45
sixth form study areas	50	80	30	–	–	–	–	–	–	–	–	–	–	can vary	80
librarian and Head of sixth form offices	–	8	–	1	8	1	8	1	8	1	8	1	8	1	8
central stock and library stores	–	6	–		12		12		12		12	add	5	add	5
chair store(s)	–	varies	–		18		18		18		18	add	6	add	6
secure/exam/community stores	–	8	–	2	16	2	16	2	16	2	16	1	8	1	8
dining area (hot meals)	N/4	varies	–	can vary	215	can vary	205	can vary	200	can vary	240	can vary	90	can vary	90
social and sandwich area(s)	varies	varies	–	can vary	35	–	–	can vary	70	–	–	can vary	95	can vary	105
kitchen (incl staff and stores)	–	101	–	1	101	1	101	1	101	1	101	add	25	add	25
Inclusion Support															
SEN resource base (case conference/tutorial)	18	20	–	1	20	1	20	1	20	1	20	–	–	–	–
small group room (SEN etc)	6	16	–	1	16	1	16	1	16	1	16	–	–	–	–
SEN therapy/MI room	4	18	–	1	18	1	18	1	18	1	18	–	–	–	–
SENco office	–	8	–	1	8	1	8	1	8	1	8	–	–	–	–
SENco/wheelchair/appliances storage	–	12	–	1	12	1	12	1	12	1	12	add	4	add	4
hygiene facilities (incl. shower)	–	30	–	can vary	30	can vary	30	can vary	30	can vary	30	–	–	–	–
Administration															
head's office	–	12	–	1	12	1	12	1	12	1	12	–	–	–	–
meeting room	–	16	–	1	16	1	16	1	16	1	16	–	–	–	–
senior management offices	–	8	–	4	32	4	32	4	32	4	32	–	–	–	–
general office	–	48	–	1	48	1	48	1	48	1	48	add	6	add	6
entrance/reception and adjacent sick bay	–	16	–	1	16	1	16	1	16	1	16	–	–	–	–
staff room (social)	–	varies	–	1	60	1	60	1	60	1	60	add	20	add	25
reprographics	–	varies	–	1	26	1	26	1	26	1	26	–	–	–	–
community and other offices	–	8	–	6	48	4	32	6	48	5	40	1	8	1	8
Other															
maintenance store(s)	–	8	–	1	8	1	8	1	8	1	8	add	4	add	4
cleaners' stores	–	1.5	–	6	9	6	9	6	9	6	9	2	3	2	3
lockers for personal storage	–	–	–	–	63	–	63	–	63	–	63	–	15	–	20
community lockers (out of school hours)	–	–	–	4	–	4	–	4	–	4	–	–	–	–	–
pupil toilets (incl. accessible cubicles)	–	2.7	–	varies	129	varies	129	varies	129	varies	129	varies	30	varies	30
staff toilets	–	3.5	–	varies	32	varies	32	varies	32	varies	32	varies	21	varies	21
total timetabled spaces				42		43		44		45		13		17	
total basic teaching					2956		2969		3048		3142		924		904
total halls					1024		1054		904		874		65		65
total learning resources					347		355		385		361		161		167
Total Teaching Area					4327		4378		4337		4377		1150		1126
total staff and administration					440		424		440		440		77		82
total storage					511		522		481		471		115		113
total dining and social					250		205		270		240		185		195
circulation — assuming net as 70% of gross					1520		1520		1520		1520		420		420
plant — not including server					152		152		152		152		45		45
partitions					247		247		247		247		71		71
Total Gross Area					7881		7890		7881		7881		2179		2178

(net 70.1% of gross)

Appendix 3

Key Formulae for Middle Deemed Secondary and Secondary Schools

N = number of pupil places

Minimum Building Areas	9–13 middle schools	11–16 secondary schools	11–18 secondary schools
basic teaching	50 + 2.5N	50 + 3N	200 + 3.06N
halls	250 + 0.3N	600 + 0.3N	600 + 0.3N
learning resources	50 + 0.2N	75 + 0.25N	125 + 0.29N
staff and administration	75 + 0.24N	125 + 0.3N	125 + 0.31N
storage	100 + 0.29N	175 + 0.35N	200 + 0.36N
dining and social	25 + 0.1N	25 + 0.2N	100 + 0.26N
'float'	150 + 0.17N	250 + 0.3N	250 + 0.32N
TOTAL NET BUILDING AREA	**700 + 3.8N**	**1300 + 4.7N**	**1600 + 4.9N**
LIKELY GROSS BUILDING AREA	**1000 + 5.4N**	**1850 + 6.7N**	**2250 + 7N**

Minimum Site Areas	All middle schools and secondary schools (except confined sites)	Middle and secondary schools in confined sites
pitches	10000 + 35N	provided 'off-site'
soft informal and social	800 + 2.5N	600 + 2.5N
games courts (hard surfaced)	600 + 2N	2000 (MUGA)
hard informal and social	400 + 1.5N	200 + 1N
habitat	200 + 1N	0.5N
'float'	1000 + 5N	remainder of site
TOTAL NET SITE AREA	**13000 + 47N**	**2800 + 4N minimum**
LIKELY SITE AREA: from	**14000 + 52N**	**4000 + 5N**
to	**16000 + 59N**	**5000 + 6N**

These formulae are the basis of the graphs later in the document. They can be used for schools where there are (approximately) the same number of pupils in each year up to Year 11. Gross area figures are approximate to allow an easy 'rule of thumb'. The stay-on rate is assumed to be 62.5% in the 11-18 schools. If the number of pupils in each year is not the same or the sixth form stay-on rate is different, the table below should be used to determine the correct formula.

Key Formulae for Calculating Building Area for Any Secondary School (except special)

	Area for each school:			Area for each pupil in:			
Minimum Building Areas	For any middle school	For any secondary school	Extra for any sixth form	KS 2	KS 3	KS 4	post-16
basic teaching	50	50	150	2.1	2.9	3.15	3.3
halls	250	600	–	0.3	0.3	0.3	0.3
learning resources	50	75	50	0.15	0.25	0.25	0.45
staff and administration	75	125	–	0.2	0.28	0.33	0.35
storage	100	175	25	0.25	0.33	0.38	0.4
dining and social	25	25	75	–	0.2	0.2	0.5
'float'	150	250	–	0.1	0.24	0.39	0.4
TOTAL NET BUILDING AREA	**700**	**1300**	**300**	**3.1**	**4.5**	**5.0**	**5.7**

Kaplan Publishing are constantly finding new v
looking for exam success and our online resou
extra dimension to your studies.

This book comes with free MyKaplan online resources so that you =
study anytime, anywhere. **This free online resource is not sold
separately and is included in the price of the book.**

Having purchased this book, you have access to the following online study materials:

CONTENT	AAT	
	Text	Kit
Electronic version of the book	✓	✓
Knowledge Check tests with instant answers	✓	
Mock assessments online	✓	✓
Material updates	✓	✓

How to access your online resources

Received this book as part of your Kaplan course?
If you have a MyKaplan account, your full online resources will be added automatically, in line with the
information in your course confirmation email. If you've not used MyKaplan before, you'll be sent an activation
email once your resources are ready.

Bought your book from Kaplan?
We'll automatically add your online resources to your MyKaplan account. If you've not used MyKaplan before,
you'll be sent an activation email.

Bought your book from elsewhere?
Go to **www.mykaplan.co.uk/add-online-resources**
Enter the ISBN number found on the title page and back cover of this book.
Add the unique pass key number contained in the scratch panel below.
You may be required to enter additional information during this process to set up or confirm your account
details.

This code can only be used once for the registration of this book online. This registration and your online
content will expire when the examinations covered by this book have taken place. Please allow one hour from
the time you submit your book details for us to process your request.

Please scratch the film to access your unique code.

Please be aware that this code is case-sensitive and you will need
to include the dashes within the passcode, but not when entering
the ISBN.

PUBLISHING

AAT

Q2022

Introduction to Bookkeeping

EXAM KIT

This Exam Kit supports study for the following AAT qualifications:

AAT Level 2 Certificate in Accounting

AAT Level 2 Certificate in Bookkeeping

AAT Certificate in Accounting at SCQF Level 6

British Library Cataloguing-in-Publication Data

A catalogue record for this book is available from the British Library.

Published by:

Kaplan Publishing UK

Unit 2 The Business Centre

Molly Millar's Lane

Wokingham

Berkshire

RG41 2QZ

ISBN: 978-1-83996-579-1

CONTENTS

Features in this exam kit

In addition to providing a wide ranging bank of real exam style questions, we have also included in this kit:

- unit-specific information and advice on exam technique

- our recommended approach to make your revision for this particular unit as effective as possible.

You will find a wealth of other resources to help you with your studies on the AAT website:

www.aat.org.uk/

Quality and accuracy are of the utmost importance to us so if you spot an error in any of our products, please send an email to mykaplanreporting@kaplan.com with full details, or follow the link to the feedback form in MyKaplan.

Our Quality Co-ordinator will work with our technical team to verify the error and take action to ensure it is corrected in future editions.

UNIT-SPECIFIC INFORMATION

THE EXAM

FORMAT OF THE ASSESSMENT

The assessment will comprise eleven independent tasks. Students will be assessed by computer-based assessment.

In any one assessment, students may not be assessed on all content, or on the full depth or breadth of a piece of content. The content assessed may change over time to ensure validity of assessment, but all assessment criteria will be tested over time.

The learning outcomes for this unit are as follows:

	Learning outcome	Weighting
1	Understand how to set up bookkeeping systems	20%
2	Process customer transactions	20%
3	Process supplier transactions	20%
4	Process receipts and payments	20%
5	Process transactions into the ledger accounts	20%
	Total	**100%**

Time allowed

1 hour and 30 minutes.

PASS MARK

The pass mark for all AAT CBAs is 70%.

 Always keep your eye on the clock and make sure you attempt all questions!

DETAILED SYLLABUS

The detailed syllabus and study guide written by the AAT can be found at:

www.aat.org.uk/

INDEX TO QUESTIONS AND ANSWERS

EXAM TECHNIQUE

- **Do not skip any of the material** in the syllabus.

- **Read each question** very carefully.

- **Double-check your answer** before committing yourself to it.

- Answer **every** question – if you do not know an answer to a multiple choice question or true/false question, you don't lose anything by guessing. Think carefully before you **guess**.

- If you are answering a multiple-choice question, **eliminate first those answers that you know are wrong.** Then choose the most appropriate answer from those that are left.

- **Don't panic** if you realise you've answered a question incorrectly. Getting one question wrong will not mean the difference between passing and failing.

Computer-based exams – tips

- Do not attempt a CBA until you have **completed all study material** relating to it.

- On the AAT website there is a CBA demonstration. It is **ESSENTIAL** that you attempt this before your real CBA. You will become familiar with how to move around the CBA screens and the way that questions are formatted, increasing your confidence and speed in the actual exam.

- Be sure you understand how to use the **software** before you start the exam. If in doubt, ask the assessment centre staff to explain it to you.

- Questions are **displayed on the screen** and answers are entered using keyboard and mouse. At the end of the exam, you are given a certificate showing the result you have achieved.

- In addition to the traditional multiple-choice question type, CBAs will also contain **other types of questions**, such as number entry questions, drag and drop, true/false, pick lists or drop down menus or hybrids of these.

- In some CBAs you will have to type in complete computations or written answers.

- You need to be sure you **know how to answer questions** of this type before you sit the exam, through practice.

KAPLAN'S RECOMMENDED REVISION APPROACH

QUESTION PRACTICE IS THE KEY TO SUCCESS

Success in professional examinations relies upon you acquiring a firm grasp of the required knowledge at the tuition phase. In order to be able to do the questions, knowledge is essential.

However, the difference between success and failure often hinges on your exam technique on the day and making the most of the revision phase of your studies.

The **Kaplan Study Text** is the starting point, designed to provide the underpinning knowledge to tackle all questions. However, in the revision phase, poring over text books is not the answer.

Kaplan Pocket Notes are designed to help you quickly revise a topic area; however you then need to practise questions. There is a need to progress to exam style questions as soon as possible, and to tie your exam technique and technical knowledge together.

The importance of question practice cannot be over-emphasised.

The recommended approach below is designed by expert tutors in the field, in conjunction with their knowledge of the examiner and the specimen assessment.

You need to practise as many questions as possible in the time you have left.

OUR AIM

Our aim is to get you to the stage where you can attempt exam questions confidently, to time, in a closed book environment, with no supplementary help (i.e. to simulate the real examination experience).

Practising your exam technique is also vitally important for you to assess your progress and identify areas of weakness that may need more attention in the final run up to the examination.

In order to achieve this we recognise that initially you may feel the need to practice some questions with open book help.

Good exam technique is vital.

KAPLAN PUBLISHING

THE KAPLAN REVISION PLAN

Stage 1: Assess areas of strengths and weaknesses

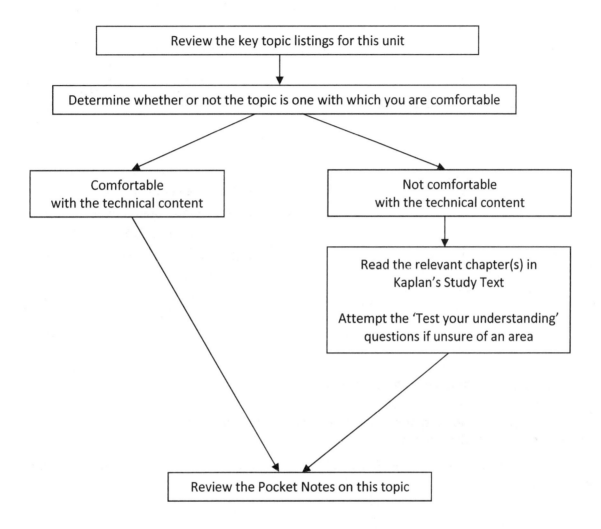

Stage 2: Practice questions

Follow the order of revision of topics as presented in this Kit and attempt the questions in the order suggested.

Try to avoid referring to Study Texts and your notes and the model answer until you have completed your attempt.

Review your attempt with the model answer and assess how much of the answer you achieved.

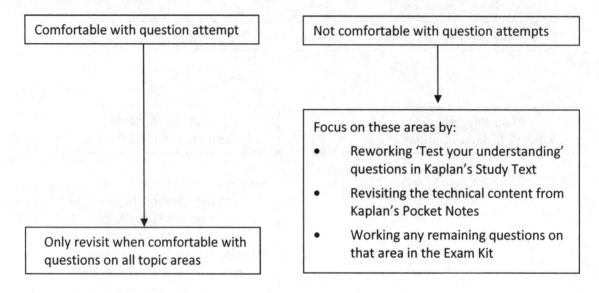

Comfortable with question attempt

Not comfortable with question attempts

Focus on these areas by:

- Reworking 'Test your understanding' questions in Kaplan's Study Text
- Revisiting the technical content from Kaplan's Pocket Notes
- Working any remaining questions on that area in the Exam Kit

Only revisit when comfortable with questions on all topic areas

Stage 3: Final pre-exam revision

We recommend that you **attempt at least one mock examination** containing a set of previously unseen exam-standard questions.

Attempt the mock CBA online in timed, closed book conditions to simulate the real exam experience.

Section 1

PRACTICE QUESTIONS

UNDERSTAND HOW TO SET UP BOOKKEEPING SYSTEMS

1   LEO LTD

Leo Ltd codes all sales invoices with a customer code AND a general ledger code. A selection of the codes used is given below.

Customer	Customer account code
DEF Ltd	DEF14
Gamma Production	GAM27
MBG Co	MBG20
Harley Interiors	HAR18
Clarkson Wholesale	CLA16

Item	General ledger code
Standard bath	GL529
Standard washbasin	GL526
Luxury taps	GL530
Bathroom cabinet	GL521
Toilet	GL535
Standard light switch	GL528

Leo Ltd	
121 Apple Lane	
Cuddington, CU9 8EF	
VAT Registration No. 398 2774 01	

DEF Ltd	
51 Neville Street,	18 Aug 20XX
Manchester, M1 4PJ	
10 .... Luxury taps for washbasin @ £8.80 each	£88.00
VAT	£17.60
Total	£105.60

(a) Select which codes would be used to code this invoice.

General ledger code	Picklist: DEF14, GL529, GAM27, GL 526, GL530, GL521, GL535, CLA16
Customer account code	Picklist: GL530, GL526, DEF14, MBG20, HAR18, GL521, GL528, GAM27

(b) Why is it useful to use a customer code?

Picklist: To help when inventory (stock) taking

To help when completing a tax return

To help find the total amount due to a supplier

To help trace orders and amounts due from particular customers

2 ELLA'S PAINTS

Ella's Paint's codes all purchases invoices with a supplier code AND a general ledger code. A selection of the codes used is given below.

Supplier	Supplier account code
Peak Ltd	PEA27
Marker Production	MAR19
MEG & Co	MEG20
Farley Interiors	FAR12
Hammond Wholesale	HAM16

Item	General ledger code
White Paint	GL360
Standard Roller	GL395
Standard Brush	GL320
Yellow Paint	GL370
Roller tray	GL330

This is an invoice received from a supplier.

<table>
<tr><td colspan="2" align="center">**Meg & Co**

12 Barker Street

Leeds L1 4NZ

VAT Registration No. 402 2958 02</td></tr>
<tr><td>Ella's Paints
19 Edmund St,
Newcastle, NE6 5DJ</td><td>18 Feb 20XX</td></tr>
<tr><td>20 .... standard rollers @ £2.30 each</td><td>£46.00</td></tr>
<tr><td>VAT</td><td>£9.20</td></tr>
<tr><td>Total</td><td>£55.20</td></tr>
</table>

(a) **Select which codes would be used to code this invoice.**

General ledger code	Picklist: PEA27, MAR19, GL360, MEG20, GL395, FAR12, GL330, HAM 16
Supplier account code	Picklist: PEA27, MAR19, GL360, MEG20, GL395, FAR12, GL330, HAM 16

(b) **Why is it useful to use a supplier code?**

Picklist: To help when inventory (stock) taking

To help when completing a tax return

To help trace orders and amounts due to particular suppliers

To help trace orders and amounts due from particular customers

3 ROBERTO & CO

Roberto & Co codes all purchase invoices with a supplier code AND a general ledger code. A selection of the codes used is given below.

Supplier	Supplier account code
Alex Ltd	ALE1
Toyworld	TOY10
Pudding and Co	PUD4
Springclean Ltd	SPR7
Spoonaway	SPO3

Item	General ledger code
Food	GL18
Toys	GL72
Stationery	GL45
Cleaning Equipment	GL78
Kitchenware	GL29

This is an invoice received from a supplier.

Alex Ltd	
Cherry Way, Haworth, BD22 9HQ	
VAT Registration No. 248 2764 00	
Roberto & Co	
Roberto House	
Ashton, AS2 8TN	1 Jan 20XX
10 .... teddy bears @ £4 each	£40.00
VAT	£8.00
Total	£48.00

(a) **Select which codes would be used to code this invoice.**

Supplier account code	Picklist: ALE1, TOY10, PUD4, SPR7, SPO3, GL18, GL72, GL45, GL78, GL29
General ledger code	Picklist: ALE1, TOY10, PUD4, SPR7, SPO3, GL18, GL72, GL45, GL78, GL29

(b) **Why is it necessary to use a general ledger code?**

[   ]

Picklist: To help when filling in a VAT return

To help when bar coding an item of inventory

To help find the total amount owing to a supplier

To help calculate expense incurred in a GL account

4 ACCOUNTING EQUATION 1

Financial accounting is based upon the accounting equation.

(a) **Show whether the following statements are true or false.**

Item	True/False
Assets less capital is equal to liabilities	
Assets plus liabilities are equal to capital	
Capital plus liabilities are equal to assets	

(b) **Classify each of the following items as an asset or a liability.**

Item	Asset or liability?
Inventory	
Machinery	
5 year loan	

5 CLASSIFICATION

Classify each of the accounts below by adjoining a line between the account and correct classification.

Accounts	Classification
Payables (PLCA)	Asset
Inventory	Income
Commission received	Liability

6   ACCOUNTING EQUATION 2

Financial accounting is based upon the accounting equation.

(a)   **Show whether the following statements are true or false.**

Item	True/False
Capital is equal to assets plus liabilities	
Assets less liabilities are equal to capital	
Liabilities are equal to capital plus assets	

(b)   **Classify each of the following items as an asset or a liability.**

Item	Asset or liability?
VAT owed to tax authorities	
Amounts owing to payables	
Money in the bank	

7   CAPEX

It is important to understand the difference between capital expenditure, revenue expenditure, capital income and revenue income.

Select one option in each instance below to show whether the item will be capital income, revenue income, capital expenditure or revenue expenditure.

Item	Capital income	Revenue income	Capital expenditure	Revenue expenditure
Receipt from sale of motor vehicle				
Receipts from credit sales				
Purchase of machinery				
Payment of electricity bill				
Purchase of goods for resale				

8   REVEX

It is important to understand the difference between capital expenditure, revenue expenditure, capital income and revenue income.

Select one option in each instance below to show whether the item will be capital income, revenue income, capital expenditure or revenue expenditure.

Item	Capital income	Revenue income	Capital expenditure	Revenue expenditure
Receipt from sale of machinery				
Payment of telephone bill				
Purchase of building				
Receipts from cash sales				
Receipts from receivables				

9   EXPENDITURE TYPES

It is important to understand the difference between capital expenditure, revenue expenditure, capital income and revenue income.

Select one option in each instance below to show whether the item will be capital expenditure, revenue expenditure, capital income or revenue income.

Item	Capital expenditure	Revenue expenditure	Capital income	Revenue income
Purchase of a new computer system				
Receipts from customers				
Receipt from sale of fixtures and fittings				
Payments of salaries to staff				
Purchase of cleaning materials				
Receipt of bank interest				

10   ASSET OR LIABILITY

(a)   **Classify each of the following items as an asset or a liability.**

Item	Asset or liability?
Factory building	
Money due to suppliers	
Car used in the business	

ABC Co has paid an electricity bill by cheque.

(b)   **Complete the sentence below by selecting the correct option to show how this transaction will affect the accounts of ABC Co.**

The expense electricity will **increase/decrease**; the asset of bank will **increase/decrease**.

11   ACCOUNTING EQUATION 3

Show the accounting equation by inserting the appropriate figures using the information provided below:

Note: All figures should be shown as a positive balance.

Assets and liabilities	£
Land & buildings	120,000
Cars & machinery	20,960
Amounts due from credit customers	4,900
Bank	12,500
Amounts due to credit suppliers	13,870
Loan	15,000

Assets £	Liabilities £	Capital £

12   MULTIPLE CHOICE 1

(a)   **State whether each of the following costs should be treated as capital expenditure or revenue expense.**

		Capital expenditure or revenue expense
(i)	Work to install additional, high-specification, electrical power cabling and circuits so that additional plant and equipment can become operational	
(ii)	Replacement of some loose and damaged roof tiles following a recent storm	
(iii)	Repainting the factory administration office	
(iv)	Modifications to the factory entrance to enable a large item of plant and equipment to be installed	

(b) **Which of the following statements best defines a statement of financial position?**

A   It is a summary of income and expenditure for an accounting period

B   It is a summary of cash receipts and payments made during an accounting period

C   It is a summary of assets, liabilities and equity at a specified date

D   It is a summary of assets and expenses at a specified date

(c) **The double-entry system of bookkeeping normally results in which of the following balances on the ledger accounts?**

	Debit balances:	Credit balances:
A	Assets and revenues	Liabilities, capital and expenses
B	Revenues, capital and liabilities	Assets and expenses
C	Assets and expenses	Liabilities, capital and revenues
D	Assets, expenses and capital	Liabilities and revenues

13   MULTIPLE CHOICE 2

(a) **Which of the following statements best defines a statement of profit or loss?**

A   It is a summary of assets and expenses at a specified date

B   It is a summary of cash receipts and payments made during an accounting period

C   It is a summary of assets, liabilities and equity at a specified date

D   It is a summary of income and expenditure for an accounting period

(b) **Which one of the following statements is correct?**

A   Assets and liabilities normally have credit balances

B   Liabilities and revenues normally have debit balances

C   Assets and revenues normally have credit balances

D   Assets and expenses normally have debit balances

(c) **Which one of the following statements is not correct?**

A   A credit balance exists where the total of credit entries is more than the total of debit entries

B   A debit balance exists where the total of debit entries is less than the total of credit entries

C   A credit balance exists where the total of debit entries is less than the total of credit entries

D   A debit balance exists where the total of debit entries is more than the total of credit entries

14   CHEN

(a)   Given below are a number of Chen's transactions. For each transaction, tick the relevant box to indicate whether it is a cash transaction or a credit transaction.

TRANSACTION		CASH	CREDIT
(i)	Receipt of goods worth £140.59 from a supplier together with an invoice for that amount.		
(ii)	Payment of £278.50 by cheque for a purchase at the till.		
(iii)	Receipt of a deposit of £15.00 for goods.		
(iv)	Sending of an invoice for £135.00 to the payer of the deposit for the remaining value of the goods.		
(v)	Sale of goods for £14.83, payment received by credit card.		

(b)   Given below are a number of typical transactions and balances that might be found in a business such as that run by Chen. Fill in the boxes to indicate whether the items are assets, liabilities, expenses or income.

(i)	Goods stored in the warehouse awaiting resale	
(ii)	Electricity bill paid	
(iii)	Sale of goods	
(iv)	Amounts owing from a customer	
(v)	Rent paid for the factory building	
(vi)	Amounts due to the owner	
(vii)	Amounts owed to suppliers	
(viii)	Cash held in the till	
(ix)	Machinery purchased for use in the factory	
(x)	Rent received for subletting part of the factory premises	
(xi)	Cash held in the business bank account	

15 ACCOUNT CODES

This task is about manual and digital bookkeeping systems.

Accounts need to be created for a new customer and a new supplier. Account codes follow the format shown below:

A letter C to indicate a customer account, or a letter S to indicate a supplier account.

The first 4 digits of the customer or suppliers name.

A 3 digit sequential number representing the number of customer or supplier accounts.

(a) **Enter the account codes for the new customer and new supplier.**

Date	Customer name	Customer account code
1 August	Worthington Ltd	CWORT092
4 August	Moss plc	

Date	Supplier name	Supplier account code
2 August	Morley & Sons	SMORL076
5 August	Chapman Ltd	

(b) **Identify whether the following statements regarding digital bookkeeping systems are true or false.**

Statement	True ✓	False ✓
The reconciliation between the individual payables ledger and the control account is completed automatically		
General ledger accounts need to be manually balanced off to extract a trial balance		

(c) **A sales invoice for a credit customer has been entered as a sales credit note incorrectly in the digital bookkeeping system. Identify TWO consequences of this error.**

Consequence	✓
The total sales value will be understated	
The business may despatch goods that have not been sold	
The total amount owed to payables will be understated	
The business may be paid for goods that have not been sold	
The business may pay the incorrect amount to a supplier	
The business will receive more money from a customer than they are expecting per their customer report	

(d) **Identify which document or statement would be used for each of the purposes below.**

Summarising the transactions for a period and classifying them into relevant categories of income and expenditure to show the overall profit or loss for the period	
Detailing all of the transactions with a credit customer during the period and advising a credit customer of the balance outstanding on their account	
To summarise the balances on each of the general ledger accounts in order to begin the preparation of the financial statements	
To correct an invoice that has been prepared incorrectly by overstating the value of goods supplied	

Options
Petty cash voucher
Trial balance
Statement of profit or loss
Bank statement
Invoice
Supplier statement
Credit note

16 PRINCIPLES 1

This task is about the principles of double entry bookkeeping.

At the end of the accounting period, a business had the following assets and liabilities.

Assets and liabilities	£
Motor vehicles	10,180.00
Cash at bank	4,367.45
Inventory	2,100.00
Receivables	4,589.45
Payables	8,392.48
Bank overdraft	1,536.97

(a) **Complete the table below showing the accounting equation.**

Assets £	Liabilities £	Capital £

The following business transactions have taken place:

Purchased a van for use in the business and agreed to pay the supplier at a later date.

Sold some goods to a customer for cash, making a profit on the sale.

(b) **Identify the dual effect of these transactions, by selecting the correct options for each transaction below.**

Transaction 1	
Effect	✓
Increase assets	
Decrease assets	
Increase capital	
Increase liabilities	
Decrease liabilities	

Transaction 2	
Effect	✓
Increase liabilities	
Increase capital	
Decrease capital	
Increase assets	
Decrease liabilities	

A trial balance has been extracted from a business' bookkeeping system.

(c) **Identify which side of the trial balance the following account balances would appear.**

Account balance	Debit ✓	Credit ✓
Opening inventory		
Payables		
Drawings		

17 DIGITAL BOOKKEEPING

This task is about manual and digital bookkeeping systems.

A business has started to sell a new type of product, and therefore additional general ledger codes need to be created in the digital bookkeeping system. All general ledger codes are 4 digits, and follow the format below:

- Asset codes start 0, followed by a 3 digit sequential code that represents the number of asset codes

- Liability codes start 1, followed by a 3 digit sequential code that represents the number of liability codes

- Income codes start 2, followed by a 3 digit sequential code that represents the number of income codes

- Expense codes start 3, followed by a 3 digit sequential code that represents the number of expense codes

(a) **Enter the account codes for each of the new general ledger codes below.**

Details	Ledger code		Details	Ledger code
Sales – dog food	2019		Insurance expense	3072
Sales – dog bedding			Courier expense	
Sales – dog toys			Advertising expense	

(b) **Identify the coding system used in the general ledger.**

Coding system	✓
Alphanumerical	
Alphabetical	
Numerical	

An invoice for the purchase of a motor vehicle for use within the business has been entered as motor expenses in the general ledger.

(c) **Identify TWO consequences of this error.**

Consequence	✓
Assets will be understated	
Sales will be understated	
Purchases will be understated	
Expenses will be overstated	

(d) **Identify whether the following statements about digital bookkeeping are true or false.**

Statement	True ✓	False ✓
It is not possible to post a duplicate transaction using a digital bookkeeping system		
Digital bookkeeping systems can automatically post recurring entries		
The trial balance will automatically balance using a digital bookkeeping system		

18 **PRINCIPLES 2**

This task is about the principles of double entry bookkeeping.

(a) **Classify the following items by choosing from the available options (you may use each option more than once).**

Item	
Motor vehicles	
Insurance costs	
Drawings	
Payables	

Options
Assets
Liabilities
Income
Expenses
Capital

The transactions shown below have taken place and been entered into the general ledger.

(b) **Identify the opposite effect of each transaction. You should ignore VAT.**

Transaction	Dual effect 1	Dual effect 2
Owner invests £20,000 cash into the business bank account	Increases assets	
Purchases a laptop computer for use within the business, paying in cash	Increases assets	
Makes a sale to a customer realising a profit on the sale. Customer agrees to pay at a later date	Increases capital	
Owner withdraws £10,000 cash from the business to pay for a private holiday	Decreases assets	
A credit customer pays the amount owed	Increases assets	

Options
Increases assets
Decreases assets
Increases liabilities
Decreases liabilities
Increases capital
Decreases capital

At the end of the accounting period, a business has the following account balances:

Item	Balance £
Office equipment	Unknown
Receivables	4,593.90
Cash	1,342.80
Bank loan	6,780.00
Inventory	1,030.00
Capital	3,486.70

(c) **Use the accounting equation to calculate the office equipment balance.**

£	

19 PRINCIPLES 3

(a) It is important to understand the difference between capital expenditure, revenue expenditure, capital income and revenue income.

Select one option in each instance below to show whether the item will be capital expenditure, revenue expenditure, capital income or revenue income.

Item	Capital expenditure	Revenue expenditure	Capital income	Revenue income
Purchase of computer equipment				
Receipts from credit sales				
Receipt from sale of motor vehicle (non-current asset)				
Purchase of motor vehicle				
Purchase of stationery				
Payment of rent				

(b) Show whether the following statements are true or false.

Statement	True ✓	False ✓
Assets less liabilities are equal to capital		
The business and owner are treated as two separate entities		
A debit increases an item of income		

(c) Classify each of the following items as an asset or a liability.

Item	Option	Options
Computer equipment		Assets
Petty cash		Liabilities
Money owed to suppliers		

PROCESS CUSTOMER TRANSACTIONS

20 ALESSANDRO LTD

On 1 August Alessandro Ltd delivered the following goods to a credit customer, Palermo Wholesale.

Alessandro Ltd   **8 Alan Street**   **Glasgow, G1 7DJ**   Delivery note No. 24369   01 Aug 20XX   Palermo Wholesale   **Customer account code:** AGG42   17 Zoo Lane   Dartford   DH8 4TJ   40 standard baths, product code SB05

The list price of the goods was £62.50 each plus VAT. Palermo Wholesale are to be given a 12% trade discount and a 5% discount if they pay within 5 working days.

(a) Complete the invoice below.

Alessandro Ltd
8 Alan Street
Glasgow, G1 7DJ
VAT Registration No. 398 2774 01

Palermo Wholesale   **Customer account code:**
167 Front St
Stanley
DH8 4TJ   **Delivery note number:**
     Date: 1 Aug 20XX

Invoice No: 327

Quantity	Product code	Total list price £	Net amount after discount £	VAT £	Gross £

Alessandro Ltd offers each customer a discount of 5% if they pay within 30 days.

(b) What is the name of this type of discount?

Picklist: Bulk discount, prompt payment discount, trade discount

21   HLB WHOLESALE

On 1 February Painting Supplies Ltd delivered the following goods to a credit customer, HLB Wholesale.

Painting Supplies Ltd **19 Edmund St** **Newcastle, NE6 5DJ**

Delivery note No. 46589

01 Feb 20XX

HLB Wholesale   **Customer account code:** HLB24

98 Back St

Consett

DH4 3PD

20 tins of white paint, product code SD19

The list price of the goods was £15 each plus VAT. HLB Wholesale are to be given a 10% trade discount and a 4% discount if they pay within 4 working days.

(a)   Complete the invoice below.

Painting Supplies Ltd
19 Edmund St
Newcastle, NE6 5DJ

VAT Registration No. 402 2958 02

HLB Wholesale   **Customer account code:**
98 Back St
Consett
DH4 3PD

Date: 1 Feb 20XX   **Delivery note number:**

                                                              Invoice No: 298

Quantity	Product code	Total list price £	Net amount after discount £	VAT £	Gross £

Painting Supplies Ltd offer a discount of 10% if their customers buy from them.

(b)   What is the name of this type of discount?

Picklist: Bulk discount, prompt payment discount, trade discount

22 RAJA LTD

On 1 August Raja Ltd delivered the following goods to a credit customer, Mashed Ltd.

Raja Ltd
22 Nursery Road
Keighley, BD22 7BD

Delivery note No. 472
01 Aug 20XX

Mashed Ltd   **Customer account code:** MA87
42 Moorside Court
Ilkley
Leeds, LS29 4PR

20 flower pots, product code P10

The list price of the goods was £5 per flower pot plus VAT. Mashed Ltd is to be given a 10% trade discount and a 4% early payment discount.

(a)   Complete the invoice below.

Raja Ltd
22 Nursery Road
Keighley, BD22 7BD

VAT Registration No. 476 1397 02

Mashed Ltd   **Customer account code:**
42 Moorside Court
Ilkley   **Delivery note number:**
Leeds, LS29 4PR

                                              Date: 1 Aug 20XX

Invoice No: 47

Quantity of pots	Product code	Total list price £	Net amount after discount £	VAT £	Gross £

Raja Ltd offers each customer a discount if they buy over a certain quantity of goods.

(b)   What is the name of this type of discount?

[   ]

Picklist: Bulk discount, prompt payment discount, trade discount

23   ROCKY RICARDO

On 1 December Rocky Ricardo delivered the following goods to a credit customer, Alpha Group.

Rocky Ricardo
1 Rocky Way
Middleton, M42 5TU

Delivery note No. 2132
01 Dec 20XX

Alpha Group   **Customer account code: ALP01**
Alpha House
Warwick
WR11 5TB

200 cases of product A, product code A1.

The list price of the goods was £10 per case plus VAT. Alpha Group are to be given a 10% trade discount and a 2% prompt payment discount.

(a)   Complete the invoice below.

Rocky Ricardo

1 Rocky Way

Middleton, M42 5TU

VAT Registration No. 298 3827 04

Alpha Group   Customer account code:

Alpha House

Warwick   Delivery note number:

WR11 5TB

                                              Date: 1 Dec 20XX

Invoice No: 950

Quantity of cases	Product code	Total list price £	Net amount after discount £	VAT £	Gross £

(b)   What will be the amounts entered into the sales daybook after the invoice in (a) has been prepared?

Sales daybook					
Date 20XX	Details	Invoice No:	Total £	VAT £	Net £
1 Dec	Alpha Group	950			

A cheque for £1,000 has now been received from Alpha Group which incorrectly states is full settlement of their account. Their account in the receivables ledger is shown below:

Alpha Group

Date 20XX	Details	Amount £	Date 20XX	Details	Amount £
1 Oct	Balance b/f	4,288	3 Oct	Bank	4,288
21 Nov	Invoice 123	1,500	25 Nov	Credit note 102	500
29 Nov	Invoice 189	2,000			

(c)   **Which item has not been included in the payment?**

Select your account name from the following list: Balance b/f, Invoice 123, Invoice 189, Bank, Credit note 102

(d)   An invoice has been sent to Alpha Group for £500 plus VAT of £100. A prompt payment discount of 1% has been offered for payment within 5 days.

(i)   **What is the amount Alpha Group should pay if payment is made within 5 days?**

£

(ii)   **What is the amount Alpha Group should pay if payment is NOT made within 5 days?**

£

24   **SDB**

Sales invoices have been prepared and partially entered in the sales daybook, as shown below.

(a)   **Complete the entries in the sales daybook by inserting the appropriate figures for each invoice.**

(b)   **Total the last five columns of the sales daybook.**

Sales daybook

Date 20XX	Details	Invoice number	Total £	VAT £	Net £	Sales type 1 £	Sales type 2 £
31 Dec	Poonams	105	3,600				3,000
31 Dec	D. Taylor	106		1,280		6,400	
31 Dec	Smiths	107	3,840		3,200		3,200
	Totals						

25 MAHINDRA LTD

Sales invoices have been received and partially entered in the sales daybook of Mahindra Ltd, as shown below.

(a) **Complete the entries in the sales daybook by inserting the appropriate figures for each invoice.**

(b) **Total the last five columns of the sales daybook.**

Sales daybook

Date 20XX	Details	Invoice number	Total £	VAT £	Net £	Sales type 1 £	Sales type 2 £
31 Jan	Square Ltd	3567			1,000	1,000	
31 Jan	Oval & Co	3568		1,600			8,000
31 Jan	Diamond Ltd	3569	13,200				11,000
31 Jan	Triangle Ltd	3570		1,320		6,600	
	Totals						

26 PAR FOR THE COURSE GOLF SUPPLIES

Customer invoice number 2808 is being prepared based on the following customer quotation.

Par for the Course Golf Supplies Ltd
To: Erehwon Golf Club   Date: 13 August 20XX
Customer code: EREH094
Further to your enquiry, we are pleased to provide a quotation for the supply of:
300 units of product 107:
Pack of 12 golf balls @ £5.40 each (discounted to £5.00 each for purchases of 250 units or more)
150 units of product 119:   Golf umbrellas @ £7.90 each
Plus VAT at 20%
Payment terms: 30 days from end of month of invoice.

(a) **Identify which type of discount was offered to the customer.**

Discount type	✓
Prompt payment	
Trade	
Bulk	

(b) Calculate the amounts to include on the customer invoice.

	£
Net amount after discounts	
VAT @ 20%	
Total	

(c) Enter the invoice into the digital bookkeeping system by selecting the correct menu option, and making the necessary accounting entries.

Menu option	✓
Purchases daybook	
Purchase returns daybook	
Cash book	
Sales daybook	
Sales returns daybook	
Discounts allowed daybook	
Discounts received daybook	

Date	Customer code	Customer	General ledger code	Invoice number	Net £	VAT code
13 Aug		Erehwon Golf Club	Option 1			Option 2

Option 1	✓
1001 Sales – golf equipment	
1002 Sales – golf buggies	
4001 Purchases – golf equipment	
7001 Receivables	

Option 2	✓
V0 – 0%	
V5 – 5%	
V20 – 20%	

27   LINKEES TOY MAKERS LTD

Customer invoice number 2808 is being prepared based on the following customer quotation.

Linkees Toy Makers Ltd
To: Thomas' Toys   Date: 17 May 20XX
Customer code: THOM08
Further to your enquiry, we are pleased to provide a quotation for the supply of:
150 units of product B64: Board games (assorted) @ £4.50 each
Plus VAT at 20%
Payment terms: 30 days from end of month of invoice. 5% discount if payment received within 14 days from date of invoice.

(a)   Identify which type of discount has been offered to the customer.

Discount type	✓
Prompt payment	
Trade	
Bulk	

(b)   Calculate the amounts to include on the customer invoice.

	£
Net amount after discounts	
VAT @ 20%	
Total	

(c)   Enter the invoice into the digital bookkeeping system by selecting the correct menu option, and making the necessary entries.

Menu option	✓
Purchases daybook	
Purchase returns daybook	
Cash book	
Sales daybook	
Sales returns daybook	
Discounts allowed daybook	
Discounts received daybook	

Date	Customer code	Customer	General ledger code	Invoice number	Net £	VAT code
17 May		Thomas' Toys	Option 1			Option 2

Option 1	✓
1001 Sales – toys	
1002 Sales – board games	
4001 Purchases – Inventory	
7001 Receivables	

Option 2	✓
V0 – 0%	
V5 – 5%	
V20 – 20%	
V1 – Exempt	

28 MARTA LTD

The account shown below is in the receivables ledger of Marta Ltd. A cheque for £668 has now been received from this customer.

William and Sammy Ltd

Date 20XX	Details	Amount £	Date 20XX	Details	Amount £
1 June	Balance b/f	4,250	2 June	Bank	4,250
23 June	Sales invoice 255	1,876	15 June	Sales returns credit note 98	1,208
30 June	Sales Invoice 286	2,459			

(a) **Which item has not been included in the payment?**

Picklist: Balance b/f, Sales invoice 255, Sales invoice 286, Bank, Sales returns credit note 98

An invoice is being prepared to be sent to William and Sammy Ltd for £3,890 plus VAT of £778. A prompt payment discount of 4% will be offered for payment within 10 days.

(b) **What is the amount Marta Ltd should receive if payment is made within 10 days?**

£

(c) **What is the amount Marta Ltd should receive if payment is NOT made within 10 days?**

£

29 DIAMONDS & RUBIES LTD

The following is a summary of transactions with Diamonds & Rubies Ltd, a new credit customer.

Invoice 3927, 5 August, £4,640
Credit note 96, 10 August, £980
Invoice 3964, 21 August, £1,560
Credit note 104, 28 August, £650
Cheque received, 30 August, £2,100

Complete the statement of account below.

Stavros

121 Baker St

Newcastle, NE1 7DJ

To: Diamonds & Rubies Ltd   **Date:** 31 Aug 20XX

Date 20XX	Details	Transaction amount £	Outstanding amount £
5 Aug	Invoice 3927		
10 Aug	Credit note 96		
21 Aug	Invoice 3964		
28 Aug	Credit note 104		
30 Aug	Cheque received		

30 MAX LTD

The following is a summary of transactions with Max Ltd, a new credit customer of Painting Supplies Ltd.

Invoice 4658, 5 Feb. £2,560
Invoice 3964, 11 Feb, £3,290
Credit note 125, 21 Feb, £230
Credit note 139, 23 Feb, £560
Cheque received, 27 Feb, £1,900

Complete the statement of account below.

<table>
<tr><td colspan="4" align="center">**Painting Supplies Ltd**
19 Edmund St
Newcastle, NE6 5DJ</td></tr>
<tr><td colspan="2">**To:** Max Ltd</td><td colspan="2" align="right">**Date:** 28 Feb 20XX</td></tr>
<tr><td>**Date
20XX**</td><td>**Details**</td><td>**Transaction amount
£**</td><td>**Outstanding amount
£**</td></tr>
<tr><td>5 Feb</td><td>Invoice 4658</td><td></td><td></td></tr>
<tr><td>11 Feb</td><td>Invoice 3964</td><td></td><td></td></tr>
<tr><td>21 Feb</td><td>Credit note 125</td><td></td><td></td></tr>
<tr><td>23 Feb</td><td>Credit note 139</td><td></td><td></td></tr>
<tr><td>27 Feb</td><td>Cheque received</td><td></td><td></td></tr>
</table>

31   **BETA BOARDS**

The following is a summary of transactions with Ava Ltd, a new credit customer of Beta Boards.

£350 re invoice 222 of 10 Aug

Cheque for £225 received 12 Aug

£744 re invoice 305 of 15 Aug

£339 re credit note 194 on 20 Aug

Cheque for £530 received 24 Aug

Complete the statement of account below.

<table>
<tr><td colspan="4" align="center">**Beta Boards**
3 Victoria Avenue
Troon
KA5 2BD</td></tr>
<tr><td colspan="2">**To:** Ava Ltd</td><td colspan="2" align="right">**Date:** 31 Aug 20XX</td></tr>
<tr><td>**Date 20XX**</td><td>**Details**</td><td>**Transaction amount
£**</td><td>**Outstanding amount
£**</td></tr>
<tr><td>10 Aug</td><td>Invoice 222</td><td></td><td></td></tr>
<tr><td>12 Aug</td><td>Cheque</td><td></td><td></td></tr>
<tr><td>15 Aug</td><td>Invoice 305</td><td></td><td></td></tr>
<tr><td>20 Aug</td><td>Credit note 194</td><td></td><td></td></tr>
<tr><td>24 Aug</td><td>Cheque</td><td></td><td></td></tr>
</table>

32   BELLA PUMPKIN

The following is a summary of transactions up to 31 December 20XX for Bella Pumpkin, a new credit customer of Rocky Ricardo.

£1,700 re invoice 1001 of 12 December
£2,350 re invoice 1004 of 21 December
£940 re credit note 101 of 21 December
£470 re invoice 1010 of 27 December
Cheque for £2,000 received 29 December

(a)   **Enter the transactions into the receivables ledger of Bella Pumpkin.**

(b)   **Insert the balance carried down and the balance brought down together with date and details.**

Bella Pumpkin

Date 20XX	Details	Amount £	Date 20XX	Details	Amount £

(c)   **Complete the statement of account below to be sent to Bella Pumpkin.**

Rocky Ricardo
1 Rocky Way
Middleton, M42 5TU

To: Bella Pumpkin   **Date:** 31 Dec 20XX

Date 20XX	Details	Transaction amount £	Outstanding amount £

33 LAYLA LTD

Layla Ltd received two cheques from Heba & Co totalling £3,361.26, as detailed in the remittance advices below. The customer has been offered a prompt payment discount of 5% for payment within 10 days.

Heba & Co	
Remittance advice 3671	
16 Aug 20XX	
Invoice	£
1028	473.87
1046	1,006.62
1059	462.20
Total	1,942.69

Heba & Co	
Remittance advice 3684	
22 Aug 20XX	
Invoice	£
1068	789.48
1096	629.09
Total	1,418.57

Company policy is to match each transaction with the remittance advice number to query any under or overpayment.

(a) **Allocate the amounts received by identifying the appropriate action in the customer report below. You may use each action more than once.**

Transaction type	Date	Details	Amount £	Action
Balance b/f	1 Aug 20XX		473.87	
Invoice 1046	4 Aug 20XX	Goods	1,059.60	
Invoice 1059	9 Aug 20XX	Services	462.20	
Invoice 1068	10 Aug 20XX	Goods	789.48	
Invoice 1096	14 Aug 20XX	Goods	662.20	

Action
Allocate full amount – 3671
Query underpayment
Allocate full amount – 3684
Query overpayment

Trinity Pet Products have a policy of offering customers a 5% prompt payment discount for payment within 10 days of the invoice date.

(b)   Complete the table below by calculating the amount that Trinity Pet Products should receive, assuming both customers take advantage of the prompt payment discount offered.

Customer name	Invoice number	Amount before discount £	Amount after prompt payment discount £
Oliver John & Co	387	8,345.60	
Excelsior Ltd	395	4,562.40	

Trinity Pet Products received a payment from another customer qualifying for a prompt payment discount. However, the prompt payment discount has been calculated incorrectly resulting in an underpayment.

(c)   Complete the table below by calculating the amount that should have been paid and the amount that remains outstanding.

Customer name	Prompt payment Discount %	Invoice amount £	Amount paid £	Amount that should have been paid £	Amount outstanding £
Galahad	5	7,529.40	7,093.52		

34   KLOPP & CO

Jurgen Ltd has received two cheques from Klopp & Co totalling £4,273.80, as detailed in the remittance advices below. The customer has been offered a prompt payment discount of 4% for payment within 7 days.

Klopp & Co Remittance advice 2976 17 Apr 20XX	
Invoice	£
Invoice 342	752.34
Invoice 354	475.61
Invoice 362	800.88
Invoice 371	235.68
Total	2,264.51

Klopp & Co Remittance advice 3018 24 Apr 20XX	
Invoice	£
Invoice 379	872.62
Invoice 383	649.23
Invoice 391	487.44
Total	2,009.29

Company policy is to match each transaction with the remittance advice number to query any under or overpayment.

(a) **Allocate the amounts received by identifying the appropriate action in the customer report below. You may use each action more than once.**

Transaction type	Date	Details	Amount £	Action
Balance b/f	1 Apr 20XX		752.34	
Invoice 354	2 Apr 20XX	Goods	475.61	
Invoice 362	9 Apr 20XX	Services	834.25	
Invoice 371	12 Apr 20XX	Services	245.50	
Invoice 379	13 Apr 20XX	Goods	1,051.34	
Credit note 46	14 Apr 20XX	Correction – 379	178.72	
Invoice 383	14 Apr 20XX	Goods	649.23	
Invoice 391	19 Apr 20XX	Goods	507.75	

Action
Allocate full amount – 2976
Query underpayment
Allocate full amount – 3018
Query overpayment

Henderson & Co has received a payment from a customer in full settlement of their outstanding balance. When Henderson & Co compare the amount received to the amount outstanding on their customer report, there appears to be an underpayment of £117.48.

(b) **Identify which TWO of the following would explain the reason for this underpayment.**

Reason	✓
The customer has taken a prompt payment discount of 6% that they were not entitled to, on an invoice of £1,958 before the discount.	
Henderson & Co have duplicated an invoice in their system for £96.90 plus 20% VAT.	
2 credit notes for £49.71 and £67.77 have been omitted by Henderson & Co.	
The customer has paid for £117.48 of goods that they never received.	

PROCESS SUPPLIER TRANSACTIONS

35   NAN NURSING

A supply of chocolate puddings have been delivered to Nan Nursing by Pudding and Co. The purchase order sent from Nan Nursing, and the invoice from Pudding and Co, are shown below.

Nan Nursing

22 Nursery Road

Keighley, BD22 7BD

Purchase Order No. HH72

To: Pudding and Co

Date: 15 August 20XX

Please supply 50 chocolate puddings product code 742087

Purchase price: £20 per 10, plus VAT

Discount: less 10% trade discount, as agreed.

Pudding and Co

17 Pudding Lane, Bradford, BD19 7HX

VAT Registration No. 234 7654 00

Invoice No. 428

Nan Nursing

22 Nursery Road

Keighley, BD22 7BD

20 August 20XX

50 chocolate puddings product code 742087 @ £2 each	£50
Less Trade Discount	£10
Net	£40
VAT	£ 8
Total	£48
Terms: 30 days net	

Check the invoice against the purchase order and answer the following questions.

(a)   Has the correct purchase price of the chocolate puddings been charged?   **Y / N**

(b)   Has the correct total discount been calculated?   **Y / N**

(c)   What would be the VAT amount charged if the invoice was correct?   £_____

(d)   What would be the total amount charged if the invoice was correct?   £_____

36   PIXIE PAPER

A supply of paper has been delivered to Alpha Ltd by Pixie Paper. The purchase order sent from Alpha Ltd, and the invoice from Pixie Paper, are shown below.

Alpha Ltd

121 Baker St

Newcastle, NE1 7DJ

Purchase Order No. PO1792

To: Pixie Paper

Date: 5 Aug 20XX

Please supply 50 boxes of A4 paper product code 16257

Purchase price: £10 per box, plus VAT

Discount: less 10% trade discount, as agreed.

Pixie Paper

24 Eden Terrace, Durham, DH9 7TE

VAT Registration No. 464 392 401

Invoice No. 1679

Alpha Ltd

121 Baker St

Newcastle, NE1 7DJ

9 Aug 20XX

50 boxes of A4 paper, product code 16257 @ £10 each	£500
VAT	£100
Total	£600
Terms: 30 days net	

Check the invoice against the purchase order and answer the following questions.

(a) Has the correct product been supplied by Pixie Paper? **Y / N**

(b) Has the correct net price been calculated? **Y / N**

(c) Has the total invoice price been calculated correctly? **Y / N**

(d) What would be the VAT amount charged if the invoice was correct? £_____

(e) What would be the total amount charged if the invoice was correct? £_____

37 PAINTS R US

A supply of paint has been delivered to Painting Supplies Ltd by Paints R Us. The purchase order sent from Painting Supplies Ltd, and the invoice from Paints R Us, are shown below.

Painting Supplies Ltd

19 Edmund St

Newcastle, NE6 5DJ

Purchase Order No. PO6548

To: Paints R Us

Date: 5 Feb 20XX

Please supply 20 tins of blue paint, product code 23567

Purchase price: £8 per tin plus VAT

Discount: less 5% prompt payment discount, as agreed.

Paints R Us

19 Valley Gardens, Stanley, DH5 8JJ

VAT Registration No. 421 385 602

Invoice No. 2485

Painting Supplies Ltd

19 Edmund St

Newcastle, NE6 5DJ

10 Feb 20XX

20 tins of blue paint, product code 23567 @ £8 each	£160.00
VAT	£30.00
Total	£190.00

Terms: 30 days net

Check the invoice against the purchase order and answer the following questions.

(a)   Has the correct product been supplied?   Y / N

(b)   Has the correct net price been calculated?   Y / N

(c)   Has the total invoice price been calculated correctly?   Y / N

(d)   What would be the VAT amount charged if the invoice was correct?   £_____

(e)   What would be the total amount charged if the invoice was correct?   £_____

38   MT MOTORS

MT Motors purchased goods costing £500 from Z (before VAT at 20%). Z gave MT Motors a trade discount of 20%.

(a)   **What was the net amount recognised as a purchase expense after the discount?**

   A   £480.00

   B   £400.00

   C   £600.00

   D   £333.33

(b)   **What was the VAT on purchases after trade discount?**

   A   £100.00

   B   £80.00

   C   £20.00

   D   £94.00

(c)   **Which one of the following statements best describes the purpose of a purchase order?**

   A   It is issued to a supplier to request supply of goods from them on terms specified within the order.

   B   It is issued to a customer to confirm the supply of goods to them on terms specified in the order.

   C   It is issued to a supplier as notification of payment.

   D   It confirms the price that will be charged by a supplier for goods supplied.

39   ECHO LTD

A supply of cardboard boxes has been delivered to Rocky Ricardo's by Echo Ltd. The purchase order sent from Rocky Ricardo's, and the invoice from Echo Ltd, are shown below.

Rocky Ricardo

1 Rocky Way

Middleton, M42 5TU

Purchase Order No. RR111

To: Echo Ltd

Date: 7 Dec 20XX

Please supply 1,000 widgets product code 243

Purchase price: £1 per widget, plus VAT

Discount: less 10% trade discount, as agreed

Echo Ltd

2 Walford Way, Essex, ES4 4XX

VAT Registration No. 533 8372 12

Invoice No. 123

Rocky Ricardo

1 Rocky Way

Middleton, M42 5TU

10 Dec 20XX

1,000 .... widgets product code 243 @ £1 each	£1,000.00
VAT	£200.00
Total	£1,200.00

Terms: 30 days net

(a)   **Check the invoice against the purchase order and answer the following questions.**

Has the correct discount been applied?   Y / N

How much should the trade discount amount be?   £_____

What would be the VAT amount charged if the invoice was correct?   £_____

The following invoice has been received from the credit supplier Messi Brothers.

Messi Brothers

Unit 3 Fothersway Business Park, Newcastle

VAT Registration No. 933 8982 02

Invoice No. 1365

Rocky Ricardo
1 Rocky Way
Middleton, M42 5TU

10 Dec 20XX

500 .... of product code 1872 @ £3.75 each	£1,875.00
VAT	£375.00
Total	£2,250.00

Terms: 30 days net

(b) **What will be the details and amounts entered into the daybook?**

Daybook:					
Date 20XX	**Details**	**Invoice No:**	**Total £**	**VAT £**	**Net £**
10 Dec		1365			

40 NORTH RIPONIA RAILWAY

The supplier credit note below has been received.

Gamel's Train Repairs Ltd	
To: North Riponia Railway	Date: 14 October 20XX
Credit note number: CN483	£
Correction of invoice no: 1859	476.50
VAT @ 20%	95.30
Total	571.80

(a)   Identify the daybook in which the credit note will be entered.

Daybook	✓
Sales daybook	
Purchases daybook	
Cashbook	
Purchase returns daybook	
Sales returns daybook	
Discounts allowed daybook	

(b)   Complete the daybook by:

- Making FOUR entries to record the credit note

- Totalling the net, VAT and total columns.

Date 20XX	Supplier	Credit note number	Net £	VAT £	Total £
17 May	Narrow Gauge Ltd	CN869	317.60	63.52	381.12
26 June	Island of Sodor plc	CN0289	84.00	16.80	100.80
8 Aug	Topham Hatt & Co	421	98.50	19.70	118.20
13 Sep	Flying Kipper Ltd	C980	206.00	41.20	247.20
14 Oct	Gamel's Train Repairs				
		Totals			

The invoice and goods received note below relate to an incorrect invoice received by North Riponia Railway.

North Riponia Railway

Goods received note GRN462

22 January 20XX

Goods received from Ulfstead Ltd:

10 iron girders

Received as ordered

Price per unit : £1,000 + VAT @ 20%

Ulfstead Ltd		
To: North Riponia Railway		Date: 22 Jan 20XX
Invoice no: 9362		
Iron girders supplied	10 units @ 1,100	11,000
	VAT @ 20%	2,200
	Total	13,400

(c) **Identify TWO discrepancies in the invoice received.**

Discrepancy	✓
Date of invoice	
Product type	
Quantity of product	
Unit price	
VAT rate	
Total	

41 MARCIN & CO

The supplier invoice below has been received.

Henry's Office Supplies	
To: Marcin & Co	Date: 14 March 20XX
Invoice number: 7208	£
Supply and fit office desks × 2	584.00
VAT @ 20%	116.80
Total	700.80

(a) **Identify the daybook in which the invoice will be entered.**

Daybook	✓
Sales daybook	
Purchases daybook	
Cashbook	
Purchase returns daybook	
Sales returns daybook	
Discounts allowed daybook	

(b) **Complete the daybook by:**

- **Making FOUR entries to record the invoice**

- **Totalling the net, VAT and total columns.**

Date 20XX	Supplier	Invoice number	Net £	VAT £	Total £
8 Mar	Norris Ltd	3897	1,010.00	202.00	1,212.00
10 Mar	Sam Jones	0187	878.40	175.68	1,054.08
11 Mar	James & Sarah Ltd	402929	463.80	92.76	556.56
11 Mar	Trevor Dylis Ltd	73910	1,329.10	265.82	1,594.92
14 Mar	Henry's Office Supplies				
		Totals			

The following credit note and invoice relates to a prompt payment discount taken by Marcin & Co.

George's Printer Repairs	
To: Marcin & Co	Date: 28 March 20XX
Invoice number: 549	£
Printer repair work	675.00
VAT @ 20%	135.00
Total	810.00
Payment terms: 30 days from end of month of invoice. 2% discount if payment received within 14 days.	

George's Printer Repairs	
To: Marcin & Co	Date: 4 Apr 20XX
Credit note number: CN45	£
To adjust invoice 548 for prompt payment discount	13.50
VAT @ 20%	2.60
Total	16.10

(c)   **Identify TWO discrepancies between the invoice and the credit note.**

Discrepancy	✓
Prompt payment discount value	
VAT	
Invoice number	
Total	

42   FREDDIE LTD

Purchase invoices have been received and partially entered in the purchases daybook of Freddie Ltd, as shown below.

Novot & Co

5 Pheasant Way, Essex, ES9 8BN

VAT Registration No. 453 098 541

Invoice No. 2176

Freddie Ltd

9 Banbury Street

Sheffield

31 July 20XX

10 boxes of product code 14212 @ £400 each	£4,000
VAT	£800
Total	£4,800

Payment terms 30 days

Purchases daybook

Date 20XX	Details	Invoice number	Total £	VAT £	Net £	Product 14211 £	Product 14212 £
31 July	Box Ltd	2177			800	800	
31 July	Shrew Ltd	2175		2,400		12,000	
31 July	Novot & Co	2176					
	Totals						

(a)   Complete the first two entries in the purchases daybook by inserting the appropriate figures for each invoice.

(b)   Complete the final entry in the purchases daybook by inserting the appropriate figures from the invoice above and complete the daybook totals.

43   ALPHA LTD

Shown below is a statement of account received from a credit supplier, and the supplier's account as shown in the payables ledger of Alpha Ltd.

ABG Ltd

14 Hassle Street, Durham, DH9 7RQ

To: Alpha Ltd

121 Baker St

Newcastle, NE1 7DJ

STATEMENT OF ACCOUNT

Date 20XX	Invoice number	Details	Invoice amount £	Cheque amount £	Balance £
1 May	468	Goods	7,600		7,600
1 June		Cheque		2,500	5,100
5 June	472	Goods	4,200		9,300
12 June	478	Goods	500		9,800
22 June	486	Goods	1,680		11,480
30 June		Cheque		2,000	9,480

ABG Ltd

Date 20XX	Details	Amount £	Date 20XX	Details	Amount £
4 June	Bank	2,500	3 May	Purchases	7,600
28 June	Bank	2,000	8 June	Purchases	4,200
28 July	Purchase return	900	15 June	Purchases	500

(a)   **Which item is missing from the statement of account from ABG Ltd?**

Picklist: Cheque for £2,500, invoice 468, Invoice 472, Purchase return £900, Invoice 486, Cheque for £2,000

(b)   **Which item is missing from the supplier account in Alpha Ltd's payables ledger?**

Picklist: Invoice 468, Invoice 472, Invoice 478, Invoice 486, Purchase return £900, Cheque for £2,500

(c)   **Once the omitted items have been recorded, what is the agreed balance outstanding between Alpha Ltd and ABG Ltd?**

44   MAXIMUS LTD

Alpha Ltd sends out cheques to suppliers on the last day of the month following the month of invoice. Below is an extract from the purchases (payables) ledger of Alpha Ltd.

Maximus Ltd

Date 20XX	Details	Amount £	Date 20XX	Details	Amount £
15 July	Purchases returns credit note 252	964	1 July	Balance b/f	5,980
21 July	Purchase return credit note 258	1,218	12 July	Purchases Invoice 864	6,386
31 July	Bank	5,980			

(a)   Complete the remittance advice note below.

Alpha Ltd	
121 Baker St	
Newcastle, NE1 7DJ	
REMITTANCE ADVICE	
To: Maximus Ltd 20XX	**Date:** 31 Aug

Please find attached our cheque in payment of the following amounts.

Invoice number	Credit note number	Amount £
	Total amount paid	

(b)   Are these two statements true or false?

A remittance note is for our records only   T / F

A remittance note is sent to a supplier to advise them of the amount being paid   T / F

45   HOLLY LTD

The account shown below is in the payables ledger of AD Wholesale. A cheque for £4,770 has now been paid to this supplier.

Holly Ltd

Date 20XX	Details	Amount £	Date 20XX	Details	Amount £
			5 Jan	Balance b/f	1,500
15 Jan	Purchase return 251	540	19 Jan	Purchase invoice 3658	2,360
31 Jan	Purchase return 286	360	27 Jan	Purchase invoice 2987	1,450

(a)   **Which item has been not been included in the payment, causing it to be overstated?**

> [ ]

Picklist: Balance b/f, Purchase invoice 3658, Bank, Purchase returns 286, Purchase invoice 2987

An invoice has been received from Rickman Repairs for £860 plus VAT of £172. A prompt payment discount of 10% will be offered for payment within 30 days.

(b)   **What is the amount we should pay, if we meet the 30 days requirement?**

> £ [ ]

(c)   **How much VAT is payable if the payment is NOT made in 30 days?**

> £ [ ]

(d)   **What is the amount we should pay if payment is NOT made within 30 days?**

> £ [ ]

46   EP MANUFACTURERS

Shown below is a statement of account received from a credit supplier, and the supplier's account as shown in the payables ledger of EP Manufacturers.

KLP Ltd
19 Mussell Street, Newcastle, NE4 8JH

To: EP Manufacturers
19 Edmund St
Newcastle, NE6 5DJ

STATEMENT OF ACCOUNT

Date 20XX	Invoice number	Details	Invoice amount £	Cheque amount £	Balance £
1 Jan	468	Goods	5,200		5,200
3 Jan	458	Goods	3,600		8,800
8 Jan		Cheque		1,400	7,400
19 Jan	478	Goods	800		8,200
21 Jan		Cheque		6,500	1,700
28 Jan	488	Goods	4,350		6,050

KLP Ltd

Date 20XX	Details	Amount £	Date 20XX	Details	Amount £
8 Jan	Bank	1,400	1 Jan	Purchases	5,200
21 Jan	Bank	6,500	3 Jan	Purchases	3,600
31 Jan	Bank	1,200	19 Jan	Purchases	800

(a)   **Which item is missing from the statement of account from KLP Ltd?**

[ ]

Picklist: Cheque for £1,200, invoice 468, Invoice 478, Cheque for £6,500, Invoice 488, Cheque for £1,400

(b)   **Which item is missing from the supplier account in EP Manufacturers' payables ledger?**

[ ]

Picklist: Invoice 468, Invoice 472, Invoice 478, Invoice 488, Purchase return £900, Cheque for £2,500

(c)   **Once the omitted items have been recorded, what is the agreed balance outstanding between EP Manufacturers and KLP Ltd?**

£ [ ]

47   STANNY LTD

Ringo's Rings sends out cheques to suppliers on the last day of the month following the month of invoice. Below is an extract from the payables ledger of Ringo's Rings.

Stanny Ltd

Date 20XX	Details	Amount £	Date 20XX	Details	Amount £
13 Feb	Purchases returns credit note 198	650	1 Feb	Balance b/f	4,650
19 Feb	Purchase return credit note 154	1,250	10 Feb	Purchases Invoice 694	2,300
28 Feb	Bank	4,650	11 Feb	Purchase invoice 658	3,640

(a)   Complete the remittance advice note below.

Ringo Rings	
37 Parker Lane	
Stoke SK1 0KE	

REMITTANCE ADVICE

To: Stanny Ltd   **Date:** 31 Mar 20XX

Please find attached our cheque in payment of the following amounts.

Invoice number	Credit note number	Amount £
	Total amount paid	

(b)   Are these two statements true or false?

A remittance note is for our and the supplier's records   T / F

A remittance note is sent by a supplier confirming amounts received from them   T / F

48   **TOYWORLD**

Shown below is a statement of account received from a credit supplier, and the supplier's account as shown in the payables ledger of Hickory House.

Toyworld

18 Landview Road

Skipton

BD27 4TU

To: Hickory House

22 Nursery Road

Keighley, BD22 7BD

STATEMENT OF ACCOUNT

Date 20XX	Invoice number	Details	Invoice amount £	Cheque amount £	Balance £
1 Jan	207	Goods	2,500		2,500
8 April	310	Goods	900		3,400
9 June		Cheque		3,400	0
17 Aug	504	Goods	500		500
18 Aug	505	Goods	4,000		4,500

Toyworld

Date 20XX	Details	Amount £	Date 20XX	Details	Amount £
9 June	Bank	3,400	1 Jan	Purchases	2,500
25 June	Bank	500	8 April	Purchases	900
			17 Aug	Purchases	500

(a)   **Which item is missing from the statement of account from Toyworld?**

    [   ]

    Picklist: Invoice 207, Invoice 310, Invoice 504, Invoice 505, Cheque for £3,400, Cheque for £500

(b)   **Which item is missing from the supplier account in Hickory Houses' payables ledger?**

    [   ]

    Picklist: Invoice 207, Invoice 310, Invoice 504, Invoice 505, Cheque for £3,400, Cheque for £500

(c)   **Assuming any differences between the statement of account from Toyworld and the supplier account in Hickory Houses' payables ledger are simply due to omission errors, what is the amount owing to Toyworld?**

    £ [   ]

49 HENRY HOUSE

Henry House sends out cheques to suppliers on the last day of the month following the month of invoice. Below is an extract from the payables ledger of Henry House.

Abbies Party Ltd

Date 20XX	Details	Amount £	Date 20XX	Details	Amount £
17 July	Purchases returns credit note 27	82	15 July	Purchases Invoice 242	220
			10 Aug	Purchases Invoice 764	44

(a) Complete the remittance advice note below.

> **Henry House**
>
> **22 Nursery Road**
>
> **Keighley, BD22 7BD**
>
> **REMITTANCE ADVICE**
>
> **To:** Abbies Party
>
> **Date:** 31 August 20XX
>
> Please find attached our cheque in payment of the following amounts.
>
> | Invoice number | Credit note number | Amount £ |
> |---|---|---|
> | | | |
> | | | |
> | | | |
> | | | |
> | **Total amount paid** | | |

(b) Which of the following statements is true?

    A   The remittance advice note will be sent to the Inventory Dept to advise them inventory has been paid for

    B   The remittance advice note will be sent to the customer to advise them of the amount being paid

    C   The remittance advice note will be sent to Henry House's bank to confirm payment is to be made

    D   The remittance advice note will be sent to the supplier to advise them of the amount being paid

50 GREY GARAGES

Grey Garages makes payments to suppliers by BACS on the 25th of every month and includes all items that have been outstanding for more than 10 days.

Below is a pre-printed remittance advice slip taken from a statement of account received from a supplier, Mulberry Motors, showing all items outstanding.

Complete the remittance advice ready for the next payment to Mulberry Motors.

Remittance advice

To: Mulberry Motors

From: Grey Garages

Payment method: **Date of payment:**

Items outstanding			Tick if included in payment
Date 20XX	Details	Amount £	
23-Jun	Invoice 213	740	
06-Jul	Credit note 14	120	
13-Jul	Invoice 216	620	
19-Jul	Invoice 257	870	
	Total amount paid		£

51 ERRICO

The two invoices below were received on 5 June from credit suppliers who offer prompt payment discounts.

Invoices:

Giacomo
VAT registration 446 1552 01
Invoice number 1923

To: Errico	4 June 20XX
	£
4 product code 45 @ £14.50 each	58.00
VAT @ 20%	11.60
	———
Total	69.60

Terms: 3% prompt payment discount if payment is received within 7 days of the invoice date.

Gaetani
VAT registration 446 4742 01
Invoice number 4578

To: Errico	4 June 20XX
	£
3 product code 42a @ £11.50 each	34.50
VAT @ 20%	6.90
	———
Total	41.40

Terms: 5% prompt payment discount if payment is received within 5 days of the invoice date.

Calculate the amount to be paid to each supplier if the prompt payment discount is taken and show the date by which the supplier should receive the payment.

Supplier	£	Date by which the payment should be received by the supplier
Giacomo		
Gaetani		

52 LEVIN & CO

The two invoices below were received on 20 October from credit suppliers of Levin & Co who offer prompt payment discounts.

Invoices:

Bridge Brothers

VAT registration 446 4752 01

Invoice number 193

To: Levin & Co   19 October 20XX

	£
5 product code 895 @ £18.75 each	93.75
VAT @ 20%	18.75
	———
Total	112.50

Terms: 2% prompt payment discount if payment is received within 4 days of the invoice date.

Mitchells

VAT registration 446 4742 01

Invoice number 578

To: Levin & Co   19 October 20XX

	£
9 product code 756 @ £13.25 each	119.25
VAT @ 20%	23.85
	———
Total	143.10

Terms: 10% prompt payment discount if payment is received within 5 days of the invoice date.

(a) **Calculate the amount to be paid to each supplier if the prompt payment discount is taken and show the date by which the supplier should receive the payment.**

Supplier	£	Date by which the payment should be received by the supplier
Bridge Brothers		
Mitchells		

It is the policy of Levin & Co to check each supplier statement as they arrive to ensure that they agree to the individual accounts within the payables ledger. Provided below is the statement of account from Xcess Stock and their account in the payables ledger.

Levin & Co's policy is to only pay for items from the supplier statement which appear in their account in the payables ledger.

(b) Place a tick next to the 3 items in the supplier statement which will not be included within the payment.

Date 20XX	Details	Amount £	Date 20XX	Details	Amount £
21 Dec	Credit note 101	940	12 Dec	Invoice 1001	1,700
			21 Dec	Invoice 1004	2,350
31 Dec	Balance c/d	3,580	27 Dec	Invoice 1010	470
		4,520			4,520
			20XY 1 Jan	Balance b/d	3,580

Xcess Stock **Unit 7 Windy Industrial Estate** **Irvine, KA6 8HU**			**Not to be paid** ✓
To: Lewin & Co			
Date: 31 Dec 20XX			
Date 20XX	Details	Transaction amount £	
12 Dec	Invoice 1001	1,700	
13 Dec	Invoice 1003	1,500	
21 Dec	Invoice 1004	2,350	
21 Dec	Credit note 101	940	
22 Dec	Invoice 1005	450	
27 Dec	Invoice 1010	470	
28 Dec	Credit note 102	50	

(c) What will be the amount paid to Xcess Stock by Levin & Co?

£

(d) One of the accounts within the payables ledger of Levin & Co is for the credit supplier Minto Madness. A credit note for a prompt payment discount of £20 plus VAT has been received from Minto Madness. Before processing the credit note, the balance on the account of Minto Madness is £1,540.

What is the amount remaining on the account taking into consideration the credit note?

£

53 KINSHASA LTD

It is company policy at Kinshasa Ltd to only take advantage of prompt payment discount if the discount percentage is at least 5%. Below is a report from the digital bookkeeping system dated today, 13 January.

Supplier account code	Supplier name	Payment terms
K17	Kennack & Co	30 days
B07	Butterworth & Sons	30 days (4% discount for payments within 10 days)
J04	Jermyn Ltd	30 days (5% discount for payments within 7 days)

(a) **Identify the amount to be paid and the date by which the supplier should receive payment, for each of the invoices below:**

Supplier name	Invoice amount £	Invoice date 20XX	Amount to be paid £	Date by which supplier should receive payment
Kennack & Co	756.90	9 Jan		
Butterworth & Sons	1,317.83	11 Jan		
Jermyn Ltd	847.60	10 Jan		

Below is a statement of account from a supplier, as well as a supplier report from the digital bookkeeping system.

Farfield Ltd Statement of Account		
To: Kinshasa Ltd		30 June 20XX
Date 20XX	Transactions	£
1 June	Opening balance	639
4 June	Invoice 287	1,204
8 June	Invoice 294	897
11 June	Invoice 304	3,453
12 June	Invoice 307	257
18 June	Credit note 045	564
26 June	Invoice 342	1,865

Supplier report		
Farfield Ltd	Supplier code F009	
Date 20XX	Details	£
1 June	Opening balance	639
4 June	Invoice 287	1,204
8 June	Invoice 294	897
11 June	Invoice 304	3,453
12 June	Invoice 307	257
12 June	Invoice 307	257
18 June	Credit note 045	564
26 June	Invoice 342	1,865
30 June	CHQ 3672	5,296

(b) Identify which THREE transactions shown on the supplier statement of account have already been paid.

Transactions	✓
Opening balance	
Invoice 287	
Invoice 294	
Invoice 304	
Invoice 307	
Invoice 307	
Credit note 045	
Invoice 342	

(c)   **Identify the type of error shown on the supplier report on the 12 June.**

Type of error	✓
Underpayment	
Overpayment	
Missing transactions	
Duplicate transaction	
Timing difference	

54   FARFIELD LTD

It is company policy at Farfield Ltd to always take advantage of prompt payment discount offered. Below is a report from the digital bookkeeping system dated today, 28 August.

Supplier account code	Supplier name	Payment terms
A09	Archer Joinery	Net monthly
S06	Sankey Electrical	2.5% discount for payments within 14 days
P05	Pannal Construction	3% discount for payments within 10 days

(a)   **Identify the amount to be paid and the date by which the supplier should receive payment, for each of the invoices below:**

Supplier name	Invoice amount £	Invoice date 20XX	Amount to be paid £	Date by which supplier should receive payment
Archer Joinery	1,340.00	25 Aug		
Sankey Electrical	4,372.80	26 Aug		
Pannal Construction	3,720.00	26 Aug		

Below is a statement of account from a supplier, as well as a supplier report from the digital bookkeeping system.

Kelham Builders Statement of Account		
To: Farfield Ltd		**31 Oct 20XX**
Date 20XX	**Transactions**	**£**
1 Oct	Opening balance	2,056
2 Oct	CHQ 0786	896
7 Oct	Invoice 308	945
10 Oct	Invoice 314	1,342
14 Oct	Credit note 048	897
22 Oct	Invoice 326	2,085
26 Oct	Invoice 338	451
30 Oct	Invoice 343	846

Supplier report		
Kelham Builders	**Supplier code K06**	
Date 20XX	**Details**	**£**
1 Oct	Opening balance	1,160
7 Oct	Invoice 308	945
10 Oct	Invoice 314	1,342
14 Oct	Credit note 048	897
22 Oct	Invoice 326	2,085
26 Oct	Invoice 338	451
29 Oct	CHQ 0831	1,605
30 Oct	Invoice 343	846

(b)   **Identify which THREE transactions shown on the supplier statement of account have already been paid.**

Transactions	✓
Opening balance	
Invoice 308	
Invoice 314	
Credit note 048	
Invoice 326	
Invoice 338	
Invoice 343	

(c)   **Identify the reason for the discrepancy between the opening balance on the supplier statement and the supplier report.**

Type of error	✓
Underpayment	
Timing difference	
Overpayment	
Missing transactions	
Duplicate transaction	

PROCESS RECEIPTS AND PAYMENTS

55   ABC LTD

There are five payments to be entered in ABC Ltd's cash book.

Receipts

Received cash with thanks for goods bought. From ABC Ltd, a customer without a credit account. Net £180 VAT £36 Total £216 S. Lampard	Received cash with thanks for goods bought. From ABC Ltd, a customer without a credit account. Net £220 VAT £44 Total £264 S Bobbins	Received cash with thanks for goods bought. ABC Ltd, a customer without a credit account. Net £530 (No VAT) Penny Rhodes

Cheque book counterfoils

Henley's Ltd (Payables ledger account HEN002) £4,925 000372	Epic Equipment Maintenance (We have no credit account with this supplier) £480 incl VAT 000373

(a) Enter the details from the three receipts and two cheque book stubs into the credit side of the cash book shown below and total each column.

Cash book – Credit side

Details	Cash	Bank	VAT	Payables	Cash purchases	Repairs and renewals
Balance b/f						
S. Lampard						
S. Bobbins						
Penny Rhodes						
Henley's Ltd						
Epic Equipment Maintenance						
Total						

There are two cheques from credit customers to be entered in ABC Ltd's cash book:

D. Davies   £851

E. Denholm   £450

(b) Enter the above details into the debit side of the cash book and total each column.

Cash book – Debit side

Details	Cash	Bank	Receivables
Balance b/f	1,550	7,425	
D Davies			
E Denholm			
Total			

(c) Using your answers to (a) and (b) above calculate the cash balance.

£

(d) Using your answers to (a) and (b) above calculate the bank balance.

£

(e) Will the bank balance calculated in (d) above be a debit or credit balance?

Debit/Credit

56 BEDS

There are five payments to be entered in Beds' cash book.

Receipts

Received cash with thanks for goods bought.	Received cash with thanks for goods bought.	Received cash with thanks for goods bought.
From Beds, a customer without a credit account.	From Beds, a customer without a credit account.	From Beds, a customer without a credit account.
Net £590	Net £190	Net £230
VAT £118	VAT £38	(No VAT)
Total £708	Total £228	
A. Blighty Ltd	R Bromby	Roxy Bland

Cheque book counterfoils

Burgess Ltd (Payables ledger account BUR003)	Fast Equipment Repairs (We have no credit account with this supplier)
£2,400	£96 including VAT
000101	000102

(a) **Enter the details from the three receipts and two cheque book stubs into the credit side of the cash book shown below and total each column.**

Cash book – Credit side

Details	Cash	Bank	VAT	Payables	Cash purchases	Repairs and renewals
Balance b/f						
A. Blighty Ltd						
R Bromby						
Roxy Bland						
Burgess Ltd						
Fast Equipment Repairs						
Total						

There are two cheques from credit customers to be entered in Beds' cash book:

A. Barnett £698

H. Connelly £250

(b) Enter the above details into the debit side of the cash book and total each column.

Cash book – Debit side

Details	Cash	Bank	Receivables
Balance b/f	1,175	3,825	
A Barnett			
H Connelly			
Total			

(c) Using your answers to (a) and (b) above calculate the cash balance.

£

(d) Using your answers to (a) and (b) above calculate the bank balance.

£

(e) Will the bank balance calculated in (d) above be a debit or credit balance?

Debit/Credit

57 JO'S

There are five payments to be entered into Jo's cash book.

Receipts

Received cash with thanks for good bought. From Jo's, a customer without a credit account.	Received cash with thanks for good bought. From Jo's, a customer without a credit account.	Received cash with thanks for good bought. From Jo's, a customer without a credit account.
Net £40 VAT £8 Total £48 T. Hunkin Ltd	Net £80 VAT £16 Total £96 Victoria Green	Net £455 (no VAT) B. Head Ltd

Cheque book counterfoils

Smiths Ltd (Payables ledger account SMI527) £4,250 001456	Arrow Valley Stationers (We have no credit account with this supplier) £120 (including VAT) 001457

(a) **Enter the details from the three receipts and two cheque book stubs into the credit side of the cash book shown below and total each column.**

Cash book – credit side

Details	Cash	Bank	VAT	Payables	Cash purchases	Stationery expenses
Bal b/f		19,546				
T. Hunkin Ltd						
Victoria Green						
B. Head Ltd						
Smiths Ltd						
Arrow Valley Stationers						
Total						

There are two cheques from credit customers to be entered into Jo's cash book:

J Drummond   £623

N Atkinson   £425

(b) **Enter the above details into the debit side of the cash book below and total each column.**

Cash book – debit side

Details	Cash	Bank	Receivables
Balance b/f	986		
J Drummond			
N Atkinson			
Total			

(c) **Using your answers to (a) and (b) above calculate the cash balance.**

£

(d) **Using your answers to (a) and (b) above calculate the bank balance.**

£

(e) **Will the bank balance calculated in (d) above be a debit or a credit balance?**

Debit/Credit

58   LAGOS

There are five payments to be entered in Lagos's cash book.

Receipts

Received cash with thanks for goods bought. From Lagos, a customer without a credit account. Net £800 VAT £160 Total £960 J Pumpkin	Received cash with thanks for goods bought. From Lagos, a customer without a credit account. Net £200 VAT £40 Total £240 B Row

Cheque book counterfoils

Lemon Ltd (Payables ledger account LEM002) £100 000123	**Remo Motor** (no credit account) £240 including VAT 000124	**Fencer** (Payables ledger account FEN001) £600 000125

(a)   **Enter the details from the two receipts and three cheque book stubs into the credit side of the cash book shown below and total each column.**

Cash book – Credit side

Details	Cash	Bank	VAT	Payables	Cash purchases	Motor expenses
Balance b/f		11,450				
J Pumpkin						
B Row						
Lemon Ltd						
Remo Motor						
Fencer						
Total						

There are two cheques from credit customers to be entered in Lagos's cash book:

Jeff Jolly £127

Dolly Darton £310

(b) **Enter the above details into the debit side of the cash book and total each column.**

Cash book – Debit side

Details	Cash	Bank	Receivables
Balance b/f	1,850		
Jeff Jolly			
Dolly Darton			
Total			

(c) **Using your answers to (a) and (b) above, calculate the cash balance.**

£

(d) **Using your answers to (a) and (b) above, calculate the bank balance.**

£

(e) **Will the bank balance calculated in (d) above be a debit or credit balance?**

Debit/Credit

59   MANGROVE

Three amounts have been paid as shown in the payments listing below.

Date 20XX	Supplier account code	Supplier name	Cash £	Cheque £
25 May	–	K Quick – cash supplier	£279.00 (exc VAT)	
26 May	WHIL07	Whiles Ltd – credit supplier		£1,374.00 (inc. VAT)
27 May	SASH12	Sasha and Co – cash supplier		£418.80 (inc. VAT)

Complete the credit side of the cash book by making the necessary entries.

Date 20XX	Details	Cash £	Bank £	VAT £	Cash purchases	Payables £
25 May	K Quick					
26 May	Whiles Ltd					
27 May	Sasha and Co					

60   SWAMP

Two amounts have been received as shown in the receipts listing below.

Date 20XX	Customer account code	Customer name	Cash £	Cheque £
23 Aug	BENN12	Bennett Ltd – credit customer		£2,924.40 (inc. VAT)
25 Aug	–	J Smith – cash customer	£488.80 (exc. VAT)	

(a)   **Complete the debit side of the cash book by making the necessary entries.**

Date 20XX	Details	Cash £	Bank £	VAT £	Cash sales	Receiv-ables
23 Aug	Bal b/f	1,089.70	8,539.43			
23 Aug	Bennett Ltd					
25 Aug	J Smith					

The credit side of the cash book shows that the total cash payments were £813.48.

(b)   **Calculate the cash balance.**

£	

61   QUEEN VIC

Part way through the month the petty cash account had a balance of £145.00. The cash in the petty cash box was checked and the following notes and coins were there.

Notes and coins	£
4 × £20 notes	80.00
1 × £10 notes	10.00
2 × £5 notes	10.00
12 × £1 coins	12.00
40 × 50p coins	20.00
45 × 20p coins	9.00

(a)   **Reconcile the cash amount in the petty cash box with the balance on the petty cash account.**

Amount in petty cash box	£
Balance on petty cash account	£
Difference	£

At the end of the month the cash in the petty cash box was £27.25

(b) **Complete the petty cash reimbursement document below to restore the imprest amount of £150.**

Petty cash reimbursement	
Date: 31.07.20XX	
Amount required to restore the cash in the petty cash box.	£

62 THE ARCHES

This is a summary of petty cash payments made by The Arches.

Mick's Motors paid	£20.00 (no VAT)
Stamps paid	£19.00 (no VAT)
Office Essentials paid	£22.00 plus VAT

(a) **Enter the above transactions, in the order in which they are shown, in the petty cash book below.**

(b) **Total the petty cash book and show the balance carried down.**

Petty cash book

Debit side		Credit side					
Details	Amount £	Details	Amount £	VAT £	Postage £	Travel £	Stationery £
Balance b/f	200.00					20.00	

Picklist: Amount, Balance b/d, Balance c/d, Details, Postage, Stamps, Stationery, Office Essentials, Mick's Motors, VAT, Travel

63   RAINBOW

This is a summary of petty cash payments made by Rainbow.

Colin's Cabs paid	£28.00 (no VAT)
Post Office paid	£18.00 (no VAT)
ABC Stationery paid	£32.00 plus VAT

(a)   Enter the above transactions, in the order in which they are shown, in the petty cash book below.

(b)   Total the petty cash book and show the balance carried down.

Petty cash book

Debit side		Credit side					
Details	Amount £	Details	Amount £	VAT £	Postage £	Travel £	Stationery £
Balance b/f	100.00						

Picklist: Amount, Balance b/d, Balance c/d, Details, Postage, Post Office, Stationery, ABC Stationery, Colin's Cabs, VAT, Travel

64   SOOTY AND SWEEP

Part way through the month the petty cash account had a balance of £135.00. The cash in the petty cash box was checked and the following notes and coins were there.

Notes and coins	£
2 × £20 notes	40.00
6 × £10 notes	60.00
15 × £1 coins	15.00
18 × 50p coins	9.00
12 × 20p coins	2.40
10 × 10p coins	1.00

(a)   Reconcile the cash amount in the petty cash box with the balance on the petty cash account.

Amount in petty cash box	£
Balance on petty cash account	£
Difference	£

At the end of the month the cash in the petty cash box was £5.00

(b) **Complete the petty cash reimbursement document below to restore the imprest amount of £250.**

Petty cash reimbursement	
Date: 31.07.20XX	
Amount required to restore the cash in the petty cash box.	£

65 PEREZ

This is a summary of petty cash payments made by Perez.

Ace Taxis paid	£26.00 (no VAT)
Kate's Couriers	£27.00 (no VAT)
Smiths Stationery	£38.00 plus VAT

(a) **Enter the above transactions, in the order in which they are shown, in the petty cash book below.**

(b) **Total the petty cash book and show the balance carried down.**

Petty cash book

Debit side		Credit side					
Details	**Amount £**	**Details**	**Amount £**	**VAT £**	**Postage £**	**Travel £**	**Stationery £**
Balance b/f	225.00						

Picklist: Amount, Balance b/d, Balance c/d, Details, Postage, Kate's Couriers, Smiths Stationery, Ace Taxis, Travel, VAT

66 TOMAS'S TILES

Part way through the month the petty cash account had a balance of £165.52. The cash in the petty cash box was checked and the following notes and coins were there.

Notes and coins	£
4 × £20 notes	80.00
4 × £10 notes	40.00
3 × £5 notes	15.00
18 × £1 coins	18.00
7 × 50p coins	3.50
18 × 20p coins	3.60
19 × 10p coins	1.90
6 × 2p coins	0.12

(a)   **Reconcile the cash amount in the petty cash box with the balance on the petty cash account.**

Amount in petty cash box	£
Balance on petty cash account	£
Difference	£

At the end of the month the cash in the petty cash box was £25.88.

(b)   **Complete the petty cash reimbursement document below to restore the imprest amount of £250.00.**

Petty cash reimbursement	
Date: 30.04.20XX	
Amount required to restore the cash in the petty cash box.	£

67 ROCKY RILEY

This is a summary of petty cash payments made by Rocky Riley.

Kath's Kars paid	£32.00 (no VAT)
Stamps paid	£25.00 (no VAT)
Pauline's Pens paid	£20.00 plus VAT

(a) Enter the above transactions, in the order in which they are shown, in the petty cash book below.

(b) Total the petty cash book and show the balance carried down.

Petty cash book

Debit side		Credit side					
Details	**Amount £**	**Details**	**Amount £**	**VAT £**	**Postage £**	**Travel £**	**Stationery £**
Balance b/f	175.00						

Picklist: Amount, Balance b/d, Balance c/d, Details, Postage, Stamps, Stationery, Pauline's Pens, Kath's Kars, Travel, VAT

68 MHAIRI MOTORS

Part way through the month the petty cash account had a balance of £110.00. The cash in the petty cash box was checked and the following notes and coins were there.

Notes and coins	£
5 × £10 notes	50.00
5 × £5 notes	25.00
4 × £1 coins	4.00
11 × 50p coins	5.50
75 × 20p coins	15.00
3 × 10p coins	0.30

(a) Reconcile the cash amount in the petty cash box with the balance on the petty cash account.

Amount in petty cash box	£
Balance on petty cash account	£
Difference	£

At the end of the month the cash in the petty cash box was £8.50

(b)   **Complete the petty cash reimbursement document below to restore the imprest amount of £200.**

Petty cash reimbursement	
Date: 31.07.20XX	
Amount required to restore the cash in the petty cash box.	£

69   DAINTY DESIGNS

Dainty Designs keeps an analytical petty cash book.

On 31 March there was one final petty cash payment to be recorded in the petty cash book.

An amount of £31.20 including VAT had been paid for fuel expenses.

(a)   **Calculate the VAT and net amounts to be recorded in the petty cash book.**

VAT £	Net £

Before the petty cash payment in (a) was recorded, amounts totalling £65.66 had been entered into the fuel expenses analysis column of the petty cash book.

(b)   **Calculate the total of the fuel expenses analysis column after the petty cash payment in (a) has been recorded.**

£

After all March petty cash payments had been made, an amount of £42.30 was left in the petty cash float.

On 31 March the petty cash float was topped up to £280.

(c)   **What will be the entry in the petty cash book to record this transaction?**

Details	Amount £	Debit ✓	Credit ✓

Picklist: Balance b/d, Balance c/d, Cash from bank

(d)   **What will be the entry in the petty cash book to record the closing balance on 31 March?**

Details	Amount £	Debit ✓	Credit ✓

Picklist: Balance b/d, Balance c/d, Cash from bank

On 2 April the following petty cash vouchers are ready to be recorded:

Petty cash voucher 222

2 April 20X7

Diesel

£27.00 plus VAT

Petty cash voucher 223

2 April 20X7

Lever arch files

£12.00 including VAT

(e) **What will be the total, VAT and net amounts to be entered into the petty cash book?**

Petty cash voucher	Total £	VAT £	Net £
222			
223			

70 RIVERA MOTORING

Rivera Motoring keeps an analytical petty cash book.

On 31 October there was one final petty cash payment to be recorded in the petty cash book.

An amount of £21.60 including VAT had been paid for stationery expenses.

(a) **Calculate the VAT and net amounts to be recorded in the petty cash book.**

VAT £	Net £

Before the petty cash payment in (a) was recorded, amounts totalling £15.50 had been entered into the stationery expenses analysis column of the petty cash book.

(b) **Calculate the total of the stationery expenses analysis column after the petty cash payment in (a) has been recorded.**

£

After all October petty cash payments had been made, an amount of £31.55 was left in the petty cash float.

On 31 October the petty cash float was topped up to £215.

(c)   What will be the entry in the petty cash book to record this transaction?

Details	Amount £	Debit ✓	Credit ✓

Picklist: Balance b/d, Balance c/d, Cash from bank

(d)   What will be the entry in the petty cash book to record the closing balance on 31 October?

Details	Amount £	Debit ✓	Credit ✓

Picklist: Balance b/d, Balance c/d, Cash from bank

On 2 November the following petty cash vouchers are ready to be recorded:

Petty cash voucher 120

2 November 20X7

FST Taxis

£20 (no VAT)

Petty cash voucher 121

2 November 20X7

Pens

£19.20 including VAT

(e)   What will be the total, VAT and net amounts to be entered into the petty cash book?

Petty cash voucher	Total £	VAT £	Net £
120			
121			

71   WHILES LTD

Whiles Ltd uses an imprest system for petty cash alongside an analysed petty cash book. At the end of October, the cash remaining in the petty cash float was £47.83. The total value of the petty cash vouchers was £302.17.

On 1 November the petty cash imprest amount was replenished.

(a)   Identify the correct entry required in the petty cash book to record this transaction.

Details	Amount £	Debit ✓	Credit ✓
See below			

Details	✓
Balance brought down	
Bank	
Sales	
Cash	

When reconciling the petty cash book and vouchers for November, the following was discovered:

- The sum of the petty cash vouchers is £196.22

- The total amount of petty cash expenditure recorded in the petty cash book is £216.22

(b)   Which TWO of the following could explain this discrepancy?

	✓
A missing petty cash voucher for £16.67 excluding VAT	
Cash of £20 has been stolen from petty cash	
A petty cash voucher for £20 has yet to be recorded in the petty cash book	
A petty cash transaction of £64.20 was incorrectly recorded in the petty cash book as £84.20	

Before recording the final petty cash transaction in December, cleaning expenses of £48.00 including VAT had been recorded in the petty cash book. The final petty cash payment to be recorded was a payment of £24.00 excluding VAT for cleaning expenses.

(c)   Calculate the balance in the cleaning expenses analysis column after this final transaction has been recorded.

£	

72   BAKER LTD

Baker Ltd uses an imprest system for petty cash alongside an analysed petty cash book. On 30 November there were 2 petty cash transactions left to record as follows:

A payment for window cleaning of £28.50 (including VAT)

A payment for A4 ring binders for £36.00 (excluding VAT)

Complete the petty cash book by making the necessary entries to record these transactions.

Date 20XX	Details	Cash £	VAT £	Cleaning £	Travel £	Food/drink £	Stationery £
30 Nov	Bal b/f	89.40	14.90	14.50	36.00	–	12.00
30 Nov	Window cleaning						
30 Nov	A4 binders						

73   BUTCHER LTD

A new transaction has been arranged, as shown in the note below:

We have entered into a contract today to lease a van for use in the business. The lease will be for a period of 8 months and will cost £250 per month, excluding VAT at 20%. The payments are due on the 5th of each month by standing order, beginning next month.

Please can you set up the recurring accounting entries required?

Thanks,

John Calabassas

17 April 20XX

(a) **Set up the recurring entry in the digital bookkeeping system**

Transaction type	General ledger code	Start date 20XX	End date 20XX	Frequency	Net amount £	VAT code
Bank	Option 1	Option 2	Option 3	Monthly		Option 4

Option 1	✓
7100 – Insurance	
1100 – Van non-current assets	
2000 – Bank	
7400 – Motor lease costs	

Option 2	✓
5 Jun 20XX	
5 May 20XX	
5 Nov 20XX	
5 Dec 20XX	

Option 3	✓
5 Jun 20XX	
5 May 20XX	
5 Nov 20XX	
5 Dec 20XX	

Option 4	✓
V0 – 0%	
V1 – Exempt	
V20 – 20%	
V5 – 5%	

(b) **Identify ONE effect of processing the recurring entry.**

Effect	✓
The standing order will be automatically set up to pay for the lease costs	
Entries will be posted to all relevant general ledger accounts	
Entries will be posted to the receivables ledger and all relevant general ledger accounts	

74   CHANDLER LTD

(a)   **Identify which of the following is NOT required in order to set up a recurring entry.**

Information	✓
The number of recurring transactions	
The frequency of the recurring transactions	
The total value of all recurring transactions	
The VAT rate	

A new transaction has been arranged, as shown in the note below:

We have entered into a contract today to provide maintenance services for a new customer, Stepping Stones Ltd. The contract will last for an initial 6 months, and we will receive £480 a month including VAT at 20%. The payments will be made by standing order on the 10th of every month, starting next month.

Please can you set up the recurring entry?

Thanks,

Erica Schwartz

Jan 20XX

(b) **Set up the recurring entry in the digital bookkeeping system.**

Transaction type	General ledger code	Start date 20XX	End date 20XX	Frequency	Net amount £	VAT code
Bank	Option 1	Option 2	Option 3	Monthly		Option 4

Option 1	✓
7560 – Rent expense	
1040 – Office equipment	
2000 – Bank	
4000 – Maintenance services	

Option 2	✓
10 Apr 20XX	
10 May 20XX	
10 Feb 20XX	
10 Jul 20XX	

Option 3	✓
10 Apr 20XX	
10 May 20XX	
10 Feb 20XX	
10 Jul 20XX	

Option 4	✓
V0 – 0%	
V1 – Exempt	
V20 – 20%	
V5 – 5%	

PROCESS TRANSACTIONS INTO LEDGER ACCOUNTS

75   LADY LTD

Given below is the purchases daybook for Lady Ltd.

Date	Invoice No.	Code	Supplier	Total	VAT	Net
1 Dec	03582	PL210	M Brown	300.00	50.00	250.00
5 Dec	03617	PL219	H Madden	183.55	30.59	152.96
7 Dec	03622	PL227	L Singh	132.60	22.10	110.50
10 Dec	03623	PL228	A Stevens	90.00	15.00	75.00
18 Dec	03712	PL301	N Shema	197.08	32.84	164.24
			Totals	**903.23**	**150.53**	**752.70**

You are required to:

- Post the totals of the purchases daybook to the general ledger accounts given

- Post the invoices to the payables' accounts in the subsidiary ledger provided.

General ledger

Payables ledger control account

	£		£
		1 Dec Balance b/d	5,103.90

VAT account

	£		£
		1 Dec Balance b/d	526.90

Purchases account

	£		£
1 Dec balance b/d	22,379.52		

Subsidiary ledger

M Brown

	£			£
		1 Dec Balance b/d		68.50

H Madden

	£			£
		1 Dec Balance b/d		286.97

L Singh

	£			£
		1 Dec Balance b/d		125.89

A Stevens

	£			£
		1 Dec Balance b/d		12.36

N Shema

	£			£
		1 Dec Balance b/d		168.70

76   SATO LTD

The following transactions all took place on 31 July and have been entered into the purchases daybook of Sato Ltd as shown below. No entries have yet been made into the ledger system.

Date 20XX	Details	Invoice number	Total £	VAT £	Net £
31 July	Peak & Co	1720	6,240	1,040	5,200
31 July	Max Ltd	1721	12,720	2,120	10,600
31 July	McIntyre Wholesale	1722	5,760	960	4,800
31 July	Pigmy Ltd	1723	3,744	624	3,120
	Totals		**28,464**	**4,744**	**23,720**

(a) **What will be the entries in the payables ledger?**

Account name	Amount £	Debit ✓	Credit ✓

Picklist: Peak & Co, Purchases, Receivables ledger control, Purchases returns, McIntyre Wholesale, Sales, Payables ledger control, Max Ltd, Sales returns, VAT, Pigmy Ltd

(b) **What will be the entries in the general ledger?**

Account name	Amount £	Debit ✓	Credit ✓

Picklist: Payables ledger control, Sales, Receivables ledger control, Purchases, VAT

77 SPARKY LTD

The following credit transactions all took place on 31 July and have been entered into the sales returns daybook of Sparky Ltd as shown below. No entries have yet been made in the ledgers.

Sales returns daybook

Date 20XX	Details	Credit note number	Total £	VAT £	Net £
31 July	Clarkson Ltd	150C	1,680	280	1,400
31 July	Kyle & Co	151C	720	120	600
	Totals		2,400	400	2,000

(a) **What will be the entries in the receivables ledger?**

Receivables ledger

Account name	Amount £	Debit ✓	Credit ✓

Picklist: Net, Purchases, Payables ledger control, Clarkson Ltd, Purchases returns, Sales, Receivables ledger control, Sales returns, Kyle & Co, Total, VAT

(b) **What will be the entries in the general ledger?**

General ledger

Account name	Amount £	Debit ✓	Credit ✓

Picklist: Kyle & Co, Net, Purchases, Payables ledger control, Purchases returns, Sales, Receivables ledger control, Sales returns, Clarkson Ltd, Total, VAT

78 LOUIS LTD

The following transactions all took place on 31 Jan and have been entered into the sales daybook of Louis Ltd as shown below. No entries have yet been made into the ledger system.

Date 20XX	Details	Invoice number	Total £	VAT £	Net £
31 Jan	Sheep & Co	1400	3,840	640	3,200
31 Jan	Cow Ltd	1401	11,760	1,960	9,800
31 Jan	Chicken & Partners	1402	6,720	1,120	5,600
31 Jan	Pig Ltd	1403	14,496	2,416	12,080
	Totals		36,816	6,136	30,680

(a) **What will be the entries in the receivables ledger?**

Account name	Amount £	Debit ✓	Credit ✓

Picklist: Sheep & Co, Purchases, Receivables ledger control, Cow Ltd, Purchases returns, Sales, Chicken & Partners, Payables ledger control, Sales returns, VAT, Pig Ltd

(b) **What will be the entries in the general ledger?**

Account name	Amount £	Debit ✓	Credit ✓

Picklist: Payables ledger control, Sales, Receivables ledger control, Purchases, VAT

79 TANAKA

The following credit transactions all took place on 31 Jan and have been entered into the purchase returns daybook of Tanaka as shown below. No entries have yet been made in the ledgers.

Purchase returns daybook

Date 20XX	Details	Credit note number	Total £	VAT £	Net £
31 Jan	May Ltd	230C	1,920	320	1,600
31 Jan	Hammond & Co	231C	1,200	200	1,000
	Totals		**3,120**	520	2,600

(a)   **What will be the entries in the payables ledger?**

Payables ledger

Account name	Amount £	Debit ✓	Credit ✓

Picklist: Net, Purchases, Payables ledger control, May Ltd, Purchases returns, Sales, Receivables ledger control, Sales returns, VAT, Hammond & Co, Total

(b)   **What will be the entries in the general ledger?**

General ledger

Account name	Amount £	Debit ✓	Credit ✓

Picklist: May Ltd, Net, Purchases, Payables ledger control, Purchases returns, Sales, Receivables ledger control, Sales returns, Hammond & Co, Total, VAT

80 ALEX

The following transactions all took place on 31 Dec and have been entered into the sales daybook of Alex as shown below. No entries have yet been made into the ledger system.

Date 20XX	Details	Invoice number	Total £	VAT £	Net £
31 Dec	Lou and Phil's	700	5,040	840	4,200
31 Dec	Eddie and Co	701	10,560	1,760	8,800
31 Dec	Noah's Arc	702	2,880	480	2,400
31 Dec	Alex and Freddie	703	720	120	600
	Totals		19,200	3,200	16,000

(a) **What will be the entries in the subsidiary (memorandum) ledger for receivables?**

Account name	Amount £	Debit ✓	Credit ✓

Picklist: Lou and Phil's, Eddie and Co, Noah's Arc, Alex and Freddie, Purchases, Payables ledger control, Purchases returns, Sales, Receivables ledger control, Sales returns, VAT

(b) **What will be the entries in the general ledger?**

Account name	Amount £	Debit ✓	Credit ✓

Picklist: Payables ledger control, Sales, Receivables ledger control, Sales returns, VAT

81 JESSICA & CO

The following credit transactions all took place on 31 Dec and have been entered into the purchases returns daybook as shown below. No entries have yet been made in the ledgers.

Purchases returns daybook

Date 20XX	Details	Credit note number	Total £	VAT £	Net £
31 Dec	Iona Ltd	4763	1,680	280	1,400
31 Dec	Matilda Ltd	2164	4,320	720	3,600
	Totals		6,000	1,000	5,000

(a) **What will be the entries in the payables ledger?**

Payables ledger

Account name	Amount £	Debit ✓	Credit ✓

Picklist: Iona Ltd, Matilda Ltd, Net, Purchases, Payables ledger control, Purchases returns, Sales, Receivables ledger control, Sales returns, Total, VAT

(b) **What will be the entries in the general ledger?**

General ledger

Account name	Amount £	Debit ✓	Credit ✓

Picklist: Iona Ltd, Matilda Ltd, Net, Purchases, Payables ledger control, Purchases returns, Sales, Receivables ledger control, Sales returns, VAT, Total

82 HORSEY REACH

The following transactions all took place on 31 July and have been entered into the discounts allowed daybook of Horsey Reach as shown below. No entries have yet been made into the ledger system.

Date 20XX	Details	Credit note number	Total £	VAT £	Net £
31 July	Ashleigh Buildings	145	36.00	6.00	30.00
31 July	143 WGT	146	54.00	9.00	45.00
31 July	McDuff McGregor	147	43.20	7.20	36.00
31 July	Cameron Travel	148	93.60	15.60	78.00
	Totals		226.80	37.80	189.00

(a) **What will be the entries in the general ledger?**

Account name	Amount £	Debit ✓	Credit ✓

Picklist: 13 WGT, Ashleigh Buildings, Cameron Travel, Discounts Allowed, Discounts Received, McDuff McGregor, Purchases, Payables ledger control, Sales, Receivables ledger control, VAT

(b) **What will be the entries in the subsidiary ledger?**

Account name	Amount £	Debit ✓	Credit ✓

Picklist: 143 WGT, Ashleigh Buildings, Cameron Travel, Discounts Allowed, Discounts Received, McDuff McGregor, Purchases, Payables ledger control, Sales, Receivables ledger control, VAT

83 BUTTERFLY BEES

These are the totals from the discounts received book of Butterfly Bees at the end of the month.

Total £	VAT £	Net £
427.20	71.20	356.00

(a) What will be the entries in the general ledger?

Account name	Amount £	Debit ✔	Credit ✔

One of the entries in the discounts received daybook is for a credit note received from Bella Bumps for £20 plus VAT.

(b) What will be the entry in the payables ledger?

Account name	Amount £	Debit ✔	Credit ✔

84 OLIVIA ROSE BRIDAL SUPPLIES

These are the totals from the discounts allowed book of Olivia Rose Bridal Supplies at the end of the month.

Total £	VAT £	Net £
226.80	37.80	189.00

(a) What will be the entries in the general ledger?

Account name	Amount £	Debit ✔	Credit ✔

One of the entries in the discounts allowed daybook is for a credit note sent to Bridezilla for £45 plus VAT.

(b) What will be the entry in the receivables ledger?

Account name	Amount £	Debit ✔	Credit ✔

85 GIRONDE TRADING

These are the totals of the discounts allowed daybook of Gironde Trading at the end of the month.

Total £	VAT £	Net £
492.00	82.00	410.00

(a) **What will be the entries in the general ledger?**

Account name	Amount £	Debit ✓	Credit ✓

One of the entries is for a credit note sent to Woody Woodburn for £65 plus VAT.

(b) **What will be the entry in the subsidiary ledger for receivables?**

Account name	Amount £	Debit ✓	Credit ✓

86 ROXY CAKE DESIGNS

These are the totals of the discounts allowed daybook of Roxy Cake Designs at the end of the month.

Total £	VAT £	Net £
381.60	63.60	318.00

(a) **What will be the entries in the general ledger?**

Account name	Amount £	Debit ✓	Credit ✓

One of the entries is for a credit note sent to Percy Tran for £28 plus VAT.

(b) **What will be the entry in the receivables ledger?**

Account name	Amount £	Debit ✓	Credit ✓

87   CANTAL SUPPLIES

These are the totals of the purchases returns daybook of Cantal Supplies at the end of the month.

Total £	VAT £	Net £
5,496.00	916.00	4,580.00

(a)   **Show the correct entries to be made in the general ledger by entering the correct account name and debit or credit next to each amount.**

Account name	Amount £	Debit/Credit
	4,580.00	
	916.00	
	5,496.00	

Picklist: Purchases / Sales / Sales returns / Purchases returns / Bank / VAT /Payables ledger control / Receivables ledger control / Debit / Credit

These are the totals of the sales returns daybook of Annandale Supplies at the end of the month.

Total £	VAT £	Net £
3,001.20	500.20	2,501.00

(b)   **Show the correct entries to be made in the general ledger by entering the correct account name and debit or credit next to each amount.**

Account name	Amount £	Debit/Credit
	2,501.00	
	500.20	
	3,001.20	

Picklist: Purchases / Sales / Sales returns / Purchases returns / Bank / VAT /Payables ledger control / Receivables ledger control / Debit / Credit

88   NC CLEANING SUPPLIES

These are the totals from the purchases returns daybook of NC Cleaning Supplies at the end of the month.

Total £	VAT £	Net £
318.00	53.00	265.00

(a)   **Show the entries to be made in the general ledger by selecting the correct account name and debit or credit option against each amount. You may use each option more than once.**

Account name	Amount £	Debit/Credit
	318.00	
	53.00	
	265.00	

Options: Purchases, Payables ledger control, Purchases returns, Sales, Receivables ledger control, Sales returns, VAT, Debit, Credit

These are the totals from the sales returns daybook of NC Cleaning Supplies at the end of the month.

Total £	VAT £	Net £
180.00	30.00	150.00

(b)   **Show the entries to be made in the general ledger by selecting the correct account name and debit or credit option against each amount. You may use each option more than once.**

Account name	Amount £	Debit/Credit
	150.00	
	30.00	
	180.00	

Options: Purchases, Payables ledger control, Purchases returns, Sales, Receivables ledger control, Sales returns, VAT, Debit, Credit

89 CHUGGER LTD

The following transactions all took place on 31 July and have been entered in the credit side of the cash book as shown below. No entries have yet been made in the ledgers.

Cash book – Credit side

Date 20XX	Details	VAT £	Bank £
31 July	Stationery	16	96
31 July	Photocopier repair	40	240

(a)   **What will be the entries in the general ledger?**

General ledger

Account name	Amount £	Debit ✓	Credit ✓

Picklist: Stationery, Insurance, Repairs, Payables ledger control, Receivables ledger control, VAT

The following transactions all took place on 31 July and have been entered in the debit side of the cash book as shown below. No entries have yet been made in the ledgers.

Cash book – Debit side

Date 20XX	Details	Bank £
31 July	Balance b/f	6,350
31 July	BBG Ltd	7,200
31 July	EFG Ltd	5,000

(b)   **What will be the TWO entries in the receivables ledger?**

Receivables ledger

Account name	Amount £	Debit ✓	Credit ✓

Picklist: Balance b/f, Receivables ledger control, BBG Ltd, Payables ledger control, EFG Ltd, Bank

(c) **What will be the entry in the general ledger?**

General ledger

Account name	Amount £	Debit ✓	Credit ✓

Picklist: Balance b/f, EFG Ltd Payables ledger control, Receivables ledger control, VAT, Bank, BBG Ltd

90 ITALIAN STALLIONS

The following transactions all took place on 31 Jan and have been entered in the credit side of the cash book of Italian Stallions Ltd as shown below. No entries have yet been made in the ledgers.

Cash book – Credit side

Date 20XX	Details	VAT £	Bank £
31 Jan	Printer repair	32	192
31 Jan	Paper	16	96

(a) **What will be the entries in the general ledger?**

General ledger

Account name	Amount £	Debit ✓	Credit ✓

Picklist: Repairs, Office supplies, Payables ledger control, Receivables ledger control, VAT

The following transactions all took place on 31 Jan and have been entered in the debit side of the cash book as shown below. No entries have yet been made in the ledgers.

Cash book – Debit side

Date 20XX	Details	Bank £
31 Jan	Balance b/f	5,100
31 Jan	AAG Ltd	4,000
31 Jan	HLG Ltd	3,000

(b)   **What will be the TWO entries in the receivables ledger?**

Receivables ledger

Account name	Amount £	Debit ✓	Credit ✓

Picklist: Balance b/f, Receivables ledger control, AAG Ltd, Payables ledger control, HLG Ltd, Bank

(c)   **What will be the entry in the general ledger?**

General ledger

Account name	Amount £	Debit ✓	Credit ✓

Picklist: Balance b/f, EFG Ltd Payables ledger control, Receivables ledger control, VAT, Bank, BBG Ltd

91   FELA'S FISH

The following transactions all took place on 31 Dec and have been entered in the debit side of the cash book as shown below. No entries have yet been made in the ledgers.

Cash book – Debit side

Date 20XX	Details	Bank £
31 Dec	Balance b/f	4,280
31 Dec	K and D Ltd	8,200

(a)   **What will be the entry in the receivables ledger?**

Receivables ledger

Account name	Amount £	Debit ✓	Credit ✓

Picklist: Balance b/f, Bank, Payables ledger control, K and D Ltd, Receivables ledger control

(b) **What will be the entry in the general ledger?**

General ledger

Account name	Amount £	Debit ✓	Credit ✓

Picklist: Balance b/f, Bank, Payables ledger control, K and D Ltd, Receivables ledger control

The following transactions all took place on 31 Dec and have been entered in the credit side of the cash book as shown below. No entries have yet been made in the ledgers.

Cash book – Credit side

Date 20XX	Details	VAT £	Bank £
31 Dec	Stationery	20	120
31 Dec	Postage		800

(c) **What will be the entries in the general ledger?**

General ledger

Account name	Amount £	Debit ✓	Credit ✓

Picklist: Bank, Postage, Stationery, Payables ledger control, Receivables ledger control, VAT

92 HICKORY HOUSE

Hickory House maintains a petty cash book as both a book of prime entry and part of the double entry accounting system. The following transactions all took place on 31 Dec and have been entered in the petty cash book as shown below. No entries have yet been made in the general ledger.

Petty cash book

Date 20XX	Details	Amount £	Date 20XX	Details	Amount £	VAT £	Postage £	Motor expenses £	Office expenses
31 Dec	Balance b/f	210.00	31 Dec	Stapler	6.72	1.12			5.60
31 Dec	Bank	90.00	31 Dec	Stamps	15.00		15.00		
			31 Dec	Parking	14.88	2.48		12.40	
			31 Dec	Stationery	19.20	3.20			16.00
			31 Dec	Balance c/d	244.20				
		300.00			300.00	6.80	15.00	12.40	21.60

What will be the FIVE entries in the general ledger?

General ledger

Account name	Amount £	Debit ✓	Credit ✓

Picklist: Balance b/f, Balance c/d, Bank, Stationery, Stapler, Motor expenses, Parking, Office expenses, Petty cash book, Stamps, Postage, VAT

93 MESSI & CO

Messi & Co maintains a petty cash book as a book of prime entry; it is not part of the double entry accounting system. The following transactions all took place on 31 Dec and have been entered in the petty cash book as shown below. No entries have yet been made in the general ledger.

Petty cash book

Date 20XX	Detail	Amount £	Date 20XX	Detail	Amount £	VAT £	Post exps £	Motor exps £	Office exps £
31 Dec	Op bal	100.00	Dec 31	Paper	27.33	4.55			22.78
			31 Dec	Stamps	4.50		4.50		
			31 Dec	Biscuits	6.60	1.10			5.50
			31 Dec	Parking	9.60	1.60		8.00	
			31 Dec	Cl bal	51.97				
		100.00			100.00	7.25	4.50	8.00	28.28

What will be the FIVE entries in the general ledger?

General ledger

Account name	Amount £	Debit ✓	Credit ✓

Picklist: Balance b/f, Balance c/d, Bank, Motor expenses, Paper, Parking, Petty cash control, Office expenses, Petty cash book, Stamps, Postage, VAT

94 STAVROS

Stavros maintains a petty cash book as both a book of prime entry and part of the double entry accounting system. The following transactions all took place on 31 July and have been entered in the petty cash book as shown below. No entries have been made in the general ledger.

Petty cash book

Date 20XX	Details	Amount £	Date 20XX	Details	Amount £	VAT £	Sundry expenses £	Business travel £	Postage
1 July	Balance b/f	140	31 July	Newsagent	16.20	2.70	13.50		
31 July	Bank	110	31 July	Tea and Coffee	60.00	10.00	50.00		
			31 July	Business Travel	36.96	6.16		30.80	
			31 July	Postage	16.00				16.00
			31 July	Balance c/d	120.84				
		250.00			250.00	18.86	63.50	30.80	16.00

What will be the FIVE entries in the general ledger?

General ledger

Account name	Amount £	Debit ✓	Credit ✓

Picklist: Postage, Balance c/d, Bank, Fuel, Balance b/f, Motor repair, Sundry expenses, Petty cash book, VAT, Business Travel

95 YUMMY CUPCAKES

Yummy Cupcakes maintains a petty cash book as a book of prime entry; it is not part of the double entry accounting system. The following transactions all took place on 31 July and have been entered in the petty cash book as shown below. No entries have yet been made in the general ledger.

Petty cash book

Date 20XX	Details	Amount £	Date 20XX	Details	Amount £	VAT £	Sundry expenses £	Business travel £	Postage
1 July	Op balance	150.00	31 July	Parking	15.00	2.50		12.50	
			31 July	Tea and Coffee	12.00	2.00	10.00		
			31 July	Travel	39.44	6.57		32.87	
			31 July	Stamps	4.00				4.00
			31 July	Cl balance	79.56				
		150.00			150.00	11.07	10.00	45.37	4.00

What will be the FIVE entries in the general ledger?

General ledger

Account name	Amount £	Debit ✓	Credit ✓

Picklist: Postage, Balance c/d, Bank, Fuel, Balance b/f, Motor repair, Sundry expenses, Petty cash book, VAT, Business Travel

96 OOH LA!

Ooh La! maintains a petty cash book as both a book of prime entry and part of the double entry accounting system. The following transactions all took place on 31 Jan and have been entered in the petty cash book as shown below. No entries have yet been made in the general ledger.

Petty cash book

Date 20XX	Details	Amount £	Date 20XX	Details	Amount £	VAT £	Sundry expenses £	Motor expense £	Postage
1 Jan	Balance b/f	80.00	31 Jan	Newsagent	12.30		12.30		
31 Jan	Bank	70.00	31 Jan	Post office	43.56	7.26			36.30
			31 Jan	Fuel	20.40	3.40		17.00	
			31 Jan	Tea and Coffee	27.30	4.55	22.75		
			31 Jan	Balance c/d	46.44				
		150.00			150.00	15.21	35.05	17.00	36.30

What will be the FIVE entries in the general ledger?

General ledger

Account name	Amount £	Debit ✓	Credit ✓

Picklist: Postage, Balance c/d, Bank, Motor Expense, Balance b/f, Business Travel, Sundry expenses, Petty cash book, VAT

97   LJ INTERIORS

These are the totals of the petty cash book at the end of the month.

Details	Amount £	Details	Amount £	VAT £	Stationery £	Postage £	Charitable donations £
Total	566	Totals	566	64	320	32	150

What will be the entries in the general ledger?

Account name	Amount £	Debit ✓	Credit ✓

98   KAZ KARATE CLUB

These are the totals of the petty cash book at the end of the month.

Details	Amount £	Details	Amount £	VAT £	Motor expenses £	Postage £	Insurance £
Total	386	Totals	386	31	155	20	180

What will be the entries in the general ledger?

Account name	Amount £	Debit ✓	Credit ✓

99   JACINTA INTERIOR DESIGN

The petty cash at Jacinta Interior Design is restored to £300 at the end of each week. The following amounts were paid out of petty cash during week 22:

Stationery	£42.30 including VAT at 20%
Travelling costs	£76.50
Office refreshments	£38.70
Sundry payables	£72.00 plus VAT at 20%

(a)   Complete the petty cash reimbursement document below to restore the imprest amount of £300.

Petty cash reimbursement	
Week 22	
Amount required to restore the cash in the petty cash box.	£

(b)   Which one of the following states the entries required to account for the reimbursement to the petty cash float from the bank account?

A	Dr Petty cash	Cr Bank
B	Dr Bank	Cr Petty cash
C	Dr Drawings	Cr Petty cash
D	Dr Drawings	Cr Bank

100   MARTHA

Martha maintains a petty cash book as both a book of prime entry and part of the double entry accounting system. The petty cash book below has been partly completed for the month of April.

Petty cash book

Date 20XX	Details	Amount £	Date 20XX	Details	Amount £	VAT £	Cleaning expenses £	Motor expenses £	Office expenses £
01 Apr	Bank	150.00	11 Apr	Cleaning supplies	14.88	2.48	12.40		
			12 Apr	Stationery	42.48	7.08			35.40

On 30th April there was one final petty cash payment for the month to be recorded:

Cleaning Services Ltd   £60 including VAT.

(a)   Calculate the VAT and net amounts of this petty cash payment to be recorded in the petty cash book.

VAT £	Net £

(b)   Calculate the total of the cleaning expense analysis column after taking into consideration the petty cash payment in (a).

£

(c)   After taking into consideration the transaction in (a) what will be the entry in the petty cash book to restore to the imprest level of £150.

Details	Amount £	Debit ✓	Credit ✓

Details picklist: Amount, Balance b/d, Balance c/d, Cash from bank

(d)   What is the entry made in the petty cash book to record the closing balance on 30th April?

Details	Amount £	Debit ✓	Credit ✓

Details picklist: Amount, Balance b/d, Balance c/d, Cash from bank

The following petty cash receipts need to be recorded in the petty cash book for the month of May.

98	99	100
Newark Printers	**ERJ Motor Supplies**	**Co-pop**
Printer ink	Wiper blades	Cleaning products
£17.40 including VAT at 20%.	£38.40 inclusive of VAT at 20%.	£6.00 gross of £1.00 VAT.

(e)   For each receipt identify the analysis column to be used for the payment and the amount of the transaction that should be recorded in the analysis column.

Petty cash receipt	Analysis column	Amount £
Newark Printers		
ERJ Motor Supplies		
Co-pop		

Analysis column picklist: Cleaning expenses, Motor expenses, Office expenses

101 ROLAND

The following transactions all took place on 31 July and have been entered into the discounts allowed daybook of Roland as shown below. No entries have yet been made into the ledger system.

Date 20XX	Details	Credit note number	Total £	VAT £	Net £
31 July	Aldo & Co	45	24.00	4.00	20.00
31 July	Hopley Brothers	46	36.00	6.00	30.00
31 July	Fernando's	47	25.20	4.20	21.00
31 July	Richmond Travel	48	38.40	6.40	32.00
	Totals		123.60	20.60	103.00

(a) **What will be the entries in the general ledger?**

Account name	Amount £	Debit ✓	Credit ✓

(b) **What will be the entries in the subsidiary ledger?**

Account name	Amount £	Debit ✓	Credit ✓

102 ROGER

Roger's cash book is both a book of prime entry and part of the double entry bookkeeping system. The following transactions all took place on 31 December and have been entered in the debit side of the cash book as shown below.

Cash book – Debit side

Date 20XX	Details	Cash £	Bank £
31 Dec	Balance b/f	200	2,883
31 Dec	TUV Ltd		4,000

(a) **What will be the entry in the receivables ledger?**

Receivables ledger

Account name	Amount £	Debit ✓	Credit ✓

(b) **What will be the entry in the general ledger?**

General ledger

Account name	Amount £	Debit ✓	Credit ✓

The following transactions all took place on 31 December and have been entered in the credit side of the cash book as shown below. No entries have yet been made in the ledgers.

Cash book – Credit side

Date 20XX	Details	VAT £	Cash £	Bank £
31 Dec	Entertainment	32		192
31 Dec	Insurance			240

(c) **What will be the entries in the general ledger?**

General ledger

Account name	Amount £	Debit ✓	Credit ✓

103 SAMIA & CO

Below are the totals from the credit side of the cash book at Samia and Co.

Details	Cash	Bank	VAT	Cash purchases	Payables
Totals	3,574.70	10,311.60	869.14	4,345.70	8,671.46

(a) **Select the correct entries to be made in the general ledger accounts shown below.**

Account name	Amount £	Debit ✓	Credit ✓
Cash purchases			
VAT			
Payables ledger control account			

The purchases and discounts allowed daybooks have been totalled and all amounts have been transferred to the relevant general ledger accounts.

(b) **Identify the correct entries in the payables and receivables ledger.**

Daybook	Debit ✓	Credit ✓	Payables ledger ✓	Receivables ledger ✓
Purchases				
Discounts allowed				

104 S WILLIAMS LTD

Below are the totals from the debit side of the cash book at S Williams Ltd.

Details	Cash ✓	Bank ✓	VAT ✓	Cash sales ✓	Receivables ✓
Totals	1,767.36	10,311.24	2,013.10	2,045.60	8,019.90

(a) **Select the correct entries to be made in the general ledger accounts shown below.**

Account name	Amount £	Debit ✓	Credit ✓
Cash sales			
VAT			
Receivables ledger control account			

The sales and discounts received daybooks have been totalled and all amounts have been transferred to the relevant general ledger accounts.

(b) **Identify the correct entries in the payables and receivables ledger.**

Daybook	Debit ✓	Credit ✓	Payables ledger ✓	Receivables ledger ✓
Sales				
Discounts received				

105 BROOKLYN BOATS

The following two accounts are in the general ledger of Brooklyn Boats at the close of day on 31 Dec.

(a) Insert the balance carried down together with date and details.

(b) Insert the totals.

(c) Insert the balance brought down together with date and details.

Electricity

Date 20XX	Details	Amount £	Date 20XX	Details	Amount £
01 Dec	Balance b/f	870			
12 Dec	Bank	350			
	Total			Total	

Picklist: Balance b/d, Balance c/d, Bank, Closing balance, Opening balance, Payables ledger control

Discounts received

Date 20XX	Details	Amount £	Date 20XX	Details	Amount £
			1 Dec	Bal b/f	500
			15 Dec	Payables ledger control	100
	Total			Total	

Picklist: Balance b/d, Balance c/d, Bank, Closing balance, Opening balance, Receivables ledger control

106 WIGGLE POGGLE LTD

The following two accounts are in the general ledger of Wiggle Poggle Ltd at the close of day on 31 July.

(a)   **Insert the balance carried down together with date and details.**

(b)   **Insert the totals.**

(c)   **Insert the balance brought down together with date and details.**

Discount allowed

Date 20XX	Details	Amount £	Date 20XX	Details	Amount £
01 July	Balance b/d	1,560			
14 July	Receivables ledger control account	480			
16 July	Receivables ledger control account	120			
	Total			**Total**	

Picklist: Balance b/d, Balance c/d, Bank, Closing balance, Opening balance, Receivables ledger control

Interest income

Date 20XX	Details	Amount £	Date 20XX	Details	Amount £
			01 July	Balance b/d	320
			28 July	Bank	80
	Total			**Total**	

Picklist: Balance b/d, Balance c/d, Bank, Closing balance, Opening balance, Receivables ledger control

107 PARDE CURTAINS

The following two accounts are in the general ledger of Parde Curtains at the close of day on 31 Jan.

(a) **Insert the balance carried down together with date and details.**

(b) **Insert the totals.**

(c) **Insert the balance brought down together with date and details.**

Electricity expense

Date 20XX	Details	Amount £	Date 20XX	Details	Amount £
01 Jan	Bal b/f	200			
22 Jan	Bank	250			
	Total			Total	

Picklist: Balance b/d, Balance c/d, Bank, Closing balance, Opening balance, Electricity Expense

Rental income

Date 20XX	Details	Amount £	Date 20XX	Details	Amount £
			01 Jan	Balance b/f	400
			28 Jan	Bank	600
	Total			Total	

Picklist: Balance b/d, Balance c/d, Bank, Closing balance, Opening balance, Receivables ledger control

108 BALANCES 1

The following four accounts are in the general ledger at close of day on 31 December.

Capital

Date 20XX	Details	Amount £	Date 20XX	Details	Amount £
			01 Dec	Balance b/f	5,000
			25 Dec	Bank	1,000

Fixtures and Fittings

Date 20XX	Details	Amount £	Date 20XX	Details	Amount £
01 Dec	Balance b/f	18,500	8 Dec	Journal	1,200
12 Dec	Bank	2,500			

Loan

Date 20XX	Details	Amount £	Date 20XX	Details	Amount £
31 Dec	Bank	1,650	01 Dec	Balance b/f	24,880

Drawings

Date 20XX	Details	Amount £	Date 20XX	Details	Amount £
01 Dec	Balance b/f	1,800			
20 Dec	Bank	650			

Record the totals and balances of each account in the table below by:

- inserting the balance carried down at 31 December,
- showing whether the balance carried down will be a debit or a credit, and
- inserting the total that will be shown in both the debit and credit columns after the account has been balanced.

Account name	Balance c/d at 31 December £	Debit/Credit	Total shown in both the debit and credit columns £
Capital			
Fixtures and Fittings			
Loan			
Drawings			

109 BALANCES 2

The following four accounts are in the general ledger at close of day on 31 March.

Capital

Date 20XX	Details	Amount £	Date 20XX	Details	Amount £
			01 Mar	Balance b/f	10,000
			25 Mar	Bank	5,000

Plant and Machinery

Date 20XX	Details	Amount £	Date 20XX	Details	Amount £
01 Mar	Balance b/f	8,500	8 Mar	Journal	800
12 Mar	Bank	1,250			

Loan

Date 20XX	Details	Amount £	Date 20XX	Details	Amount £
31 Mar	Bank	1,020	01 Mar	Balance b/f	15,200

Drawings

Date 20XX	Details	Amount £	Date 20XX	Details	Amount £
01 Mar	Balance b/f	3,330			
20 Mar	Bank	890			

Record the totals and balances of each account in the table below by:

- inserting the balance carried down at 31 March,

- showing whether the balance carried down will be a debit or a credit, and

- inserting the total that will be shown in both the debit and credit columns after the account has been balanced.

Account name	Balance c/d at 31 March £	Debit/Credit	Total shown in both the debit and credit columns £
Capital			
Plant and Machinery			
Loan			
Drawings			

110 BALANCES 3

The following accounts are in the general ledger at 31 December.

AD014

Date 20XX	Details	Amount £	Date 20XX	Details	Amount £
21 Dec	Bank	465	14 Dec	Cash	947
28 Dec	Bank	1,987			

AD019

Date 20XX	Details	Amount £	Date 20XX	Details	Amount £
19 Dec	Cash	136	3 Dec	Bank	948
			12 Dec	Cash	2,362

AD036

Date 20XX	Details	Amount £	Date 20XX	Details	Amount £
7 Dec	Cash	754	3 Dec	Bank	856
18 Dec	Bank	429	27 Dec	Cash	306

(a)   Identify the entries required to record the balance carried down in each account.

Account	Amount £	Debit ✓	Credit ✓
AD014			
AD019			
AD036			

The following ledger account is ready to be totalled and balanced at the end of December.

(b)   Complete the account below by inserting the following entries into the account:

- The balance carried down as at 31 December
- The totals (you may use each total more than once)
- The balance brought down as at 1 January

Receivables

Date	Details	Amount £	Date	Details	Amount £
1 Dec	Balance brought down	9,864	17 Dec	Cash	7,493
21 Dec	Sales	4,928			

Entries		
	Total	14,792
1 Jan	Balance carried down	7,299
31 Dec	Balance brought down	7,299

Section 2

ANSWERS TO PRACTICE QUESTIONS

UNDERSTAND HOW TO SET UP BOOKKEEPING SYSTEMS

1 LEO LTD

(a)

General ledger code	GL530
Customer account code	DEF14

(b)

To help trace orders and amounts due from particular customers

2 ELLA'S PAINTS

(a)

General ledger code	GL395
Supplier account code	MEG20

(b)

To help trace orders and amounts due to particular suppliers

3 ROBERTO & CO

(a)

Supplier account code	ALE1
General ledger code	GL72

(b)

To help calculate expense incurred in a GL account

4   ACCOUNTING EQUATION 1

(a)

Item	True/False
Assets less capital is equal to liabilities	True
Assets plus liabilities are equal to capital	False
Capital plus liabilities are equal to assets	True

(b)

Item	Asset or liability?
Inventory	Asset
Machinery	Asset
5 year loan	Liability

5   CLASSIFICATION

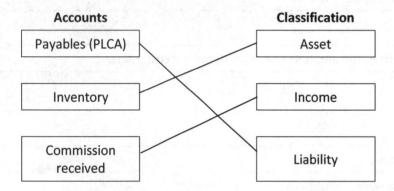

Accounts	Classification
Payables (PLCA)	Asset
Inventory	Income
Commission received	Liability

6   ACCOUNTING EQUATION 2

(a)

Item	True/False
Capital is equal to assets plus liabilities	False
Assets less liabilities are equal to capital	True
Liabilities are equal to capital plus assets	False

(b)

Item	Asset or liability?
VAT owed to tax authorities	Liability
Amounts owing to payables	Liability
Money in the bank	Asset

7 CAPEX

Item	Capital income	Revenue income	Capital expenditure	Revenue expenditure
Receipt from sale of motor vehicle	✓			
Receipts from credit sales		✓		
Purchase of machinery			✓	
Payment of electricity bill				✓
Purchase of goods for resale				✓

8 REVEX

Item	Capital income	Revenue income	Capital expenditure	Revenue expenditure
Receipt from sale of machinery	✓			
Payment of telephone bill				✓
Purchase of building			✓	
Receipts from cash sales		✓		
Receipts from receivables		✓		

9 EXPENDITURE TYPES

Item	Capital expenditure	Revenue expenditure	Capital income	Revenue income
Purchase of a new computer system	✓			
Receipts from customers				✓
Receipt from sale of fixtures and fittings			✓	
Payments of salaries to staff		✓		
Purchase of cleaning materials		✓		
Receipt of bank interest				✓

10   ASSET OR LIABILITY

(a)

Item	Asset or liability?
Factory building	Asset
Money due to suppliers	Liability
Car used in the business	Asset

(b)   The expense electricity will **increase**; the asset of bank will **decrease**.

11   ACCOUNTING EQUATION 3

Assets £	Liabilities £	Capital £
158,360	28,870	129,490

12   MULTIPLE CHOICE 1

(a)

		Capital expenditure or revenue expense
(i)	Work to install additional, high-specification, electrical power cabling and circuits so that additional plant and equipment can become operational	Capital
(ii)	Replacement of some loose and damaged roof tiles following a recent storm	Revenue
(iii)	Repainting the factory administration office	Revenue
(iv)	Modifications to the factory entrance to enable a large item of plant and equipment to be installed	Capital

(b)   **C**   It is a summary of assets, liabilities and equity at a specified date

(c)   **Debit balances:**   **Credit balances:**

      C   Assets and expenses   Liabilities, capital and revenues

13   MULTIPLE CHOICE 2

(a)   **D**   It is a summary of income and expenditure for an accounting period

(b)   **D**   Assets and expenses normally have debit balances

(c)   **B**   A debit balance exists where the total of debit entries is less than the total of credit entries

14 CHEN

(a)

	TRANSACTION	CASH	CREDIT
(i)	Receipt of goods worth £140.59 from a supplier together with an invoice for that amount.		✓
(ii)	Payment of £278.50 by cheque for a purchase at the till.	✓	
(iii)	Receipt of a deposit of £15.00 for goods.	✓	
(iv)	Sending of an invoice for £135.00 to the payer of the deposit for the remaining value of the goods.		✓
(v)	Sale of goods for £14.83, payment received by credit card.	✓	

(b)

(i) Asset – inventory

(ii) Expense

(iii) Income

(iv) Asset – trade receivables

(v) Expense

(vi) Liability (this is a special liability known as capital)

(vii) Liability – payables

(viii) Asset

(ix) Asset

(x) Income

(xi) Asset

15 ACCOUNT CODES

(a)

Date	Customer name	Customer account code
1 August	Worthington Ltd	CWORT092
4 August	Moss plc	CMOSS093

Date	Supplier name	Supplier account code
2 August	Morley & Sons	SMORL076
5 August	Chapman Ltd	SCHAP077

(b)

Statement	True ✓	False ✓
The reconciliation between the individual payables ledger and the control account is completed automatically	✓	
General ledger accounts need to be manually balanced off to extract a trial balance		✓

(c)

Consequence	✓
The total sales value will be understated	✓
The business may despatch goods that have not been sold	
The total amount owed to payables will be understated	
The business may be paid for goods that have not been sold	
The business may pay the incorrect amount to a supplier	
The business will receive more money from a customer than they are expecting per their customer report	✓

Feedback:

Item 1: Sales would have been debited rather than credited resulting in understatement. Item 2: Goods are despatched on generation of a sales order, not an invoice or credit note. Item 3: Errors over sales affects receivables rather than payables. Item 4: The business should be paid the right amount as a sales invoice was correctly sent to the customer. Item 5: The transaction invoices sales rather than purchases. Item 6: The business will have understated receivables and as a result will be paid more than they expect.

(d)

Summarising the transactions for a period and classifying them into relevant categories of income and expenditure to show the overall profit or loss for the period	Statement of profit or loss
Detailing all of the transactions with a credit customer during the period and advising a credit customer of the balance outstanding on their account	Statement of account
To summarise the balances on each of the general ledger accounts in order to begin the preparation of the financial statements	Trial balance
To correct an invoice that has been prepared incorrectly by overstating the value of goods supplied	Credit note

16   PRINCIPLES 1

(a)

Assets £	Liabilities £	Capital £
£21,236.90	£9,929.45	£11,307.45

Feedback:

Assets = £10,180.00 + £4,367.45 + £2,100.00 + £4,589.45 = £21,236.90

Liabilities = £8,392.48 + £1,536.97 = £9,929.45

Capital = Assets – Liabilities = £21,236.90 – £9,929.45 = £11,307.45

(b)

Transaction 1	
Effect	✓
Increase assets	✓
Decrease assets	
Increase capital	
Increase liabilities	✓
Decrease liabilities	

Transaction 2	
Effect	✓
Increase liabilities	
Increase capital	✓
Decrease capital	
Increase assets	✓
Decrease liabilities	

Feedback:

Transaction 1 – Dr Non-current assets, Cr Payables

Transaction 2 – Dr Cash, Cr Inventory, Cr Capital

Note: the increase in cash will exceed the reduction in inventory as the goods were sold at a profit.

(c)

Account balance	Debit ✓	Credit ✓
Opening inventory	✓	
Payables		✓
Drawings	✓	

17   DIGITAL BOOKKEEPING

(a)

Details	Ledger code		Details	Ledger code
Sales – dog food	2019		Insurance expense	3072
Sales – dog bedding	2020		Courier expense	3073
Sales – dog toys	2021		Advertising expense	3074

Feedback: As these are new general ledger codes, we can assume they will run in sequence from the first ones given in the question.

(b)

Coding system	✓
Alphanumerical	
Alphabetical	
Numerical	✓

Feedback: only numbers are used in the coding system.

(c)

Consequence	✓
Assets will be understated	✓
Sales will be understated	
Purchases will be understated	
Expenses will be overstated	✓

(d)

Statement	True ✓	False ✓
It is not possible to post a duplicate transaction using a digital bookkeeping system		✓
Digital bookkeeping systems can automatically post recurring entries	✓	
The trial balance will automatically balance using a digital bookkeeping system	✓	

Feedback:

Item 1 – the operator could post the same transaction into the system twice. Item 2 – this is a typical function of digital systems. Item 3 – Digital systems will always process matching debits and credits although may use a suspense account.

18 PRINCIPLES 2

(a)

Item	
Motor vehicles	Assets
Insurance costs	Expenses
Drawings	Capital
Payables	Liabilities

(b)

Transaction	Dual effect 1	Dual effect 2
Owner invests £20,000 cash into the business bank account	Increases assets	Increases capital
Purchases a laptop computer for use within the business, paying in cash	Increases assets	Decreases assets
Makes a sale to a customer realising a profit on the sale. Customer agrees to pay at a later date	Increases capital	Increases assets
Owner withdraws £10,000 cash from the business to pay for a private holiday	Decreases assets	Decreases capital
A credit customer pays the amount owed	Increases assets	Decreases assets

Feedback: Item 1 – This is capital introduced. Item 2 – Non-current assets increase, but cash reduces by an equivalent amount. Item 3 – Trade receivables increase by more than the reduction in inventory (as a profit has been made). Item 4 – Cash decreases and the drawings also result in a decrease in capital. Item 5 – Cash increases and trade receivables decrease by an equivalent amount.

(c)

£	3,300.00

Feedback: Assets – liabilities = Capital

Office equipment + £4,593.90 + £1,342.80 + £1030.00 – £6,780.00 = £3,486.70

Rearrange the equation:

Office equipment = £3,486.70 – £4,593.90 – £1,342.80 – £1030.00 + £6,780.00 = £3,300.00

19 PRINCIPLES 3

(a)

Item	Capital expenditure	Revenue expenditure	Capital income	Revenue income
Purchase of computer equipment	✓			
Receipts from credit sales				✓
Receipt from sale of motor vehicle (non-current asset)			✓	
Purchase of motor vehicle	✓			
Purchase of stationery		✓		
Payment of rent		✓		

(b)

Statement	True ✓	False ✓
Assets less liabilities are equal to capital	✓	
The business and owner are treated as two separate entities	✓	
A debit increases an item of income		✓

(c)

Item	Option
Computer equipment	Assets
Petty cash	Assets
Money owed to suppliers	Liabilities

PROCESS CUSTOMER TRANSACTIONS

20 ALESSANDRO LTD

(a)

Alessandro Ltd **8 Alan Street** **Glasgow, G1 7DJ** **VAT Registration No. 398 2774 01**					
Palermo Wholesale 167 Front St Stanley DH8 4TJ Invoice No: 327			**Customer account code:** AGG42 **Delivery note number: 24369** **Date:** 1 Aug 20XX		
Quantity	**Product code**	**Total list price** **£**	**Net amount after discount** **£**	**VAT** **£**	**Gross** **£**
40	SB05	2,500	2,200	440	2,640

(b)

Prompt payment discount

21 HLB WHOLESALE

(a)

Painting Supplies Ltd **19 Edmund St** **Newcastle, NE6 5DJ** **VAT Registration No. 402 2958 02**					
HLB Wholesale 98 Back St Consett DH4 3PD **Date:** 1 Feb 20XX			**Customer account code:** HLB24 **Delivery note number: 46589** **Invoice No:** 298		
Quantity	**Product code**	**Total list price** **£**	**Net amount after discount** **£**	**VAT** **£**	**Gross** **£**
20	SD19	300	270	54	324

(b)

Trade discount

22   **RAJA LTD**

   (a)

Raja Ltd					
22 Nursery Road					
Keighley, BD22 7BD					
VAT Registration No. 476 1397 02					

Mashed Ltd   **Customer account code: MA87**
42 Moorside Court
Ilkley   **Delivery note number: 472**
Leeds, LS29 4PR

                                         Date: 1 Aug 20XX

Invoice No: 47

Quantity of pots	Product code	Total list price £	Net amount after discount £	VAT £	Gross £
20	P10	100	90	18	108

   (b)

Bulk discount

23   **ROCKY RICARDO**

   (a)

Rocky Ricardo					
1 Rocky Way					
Middleton, M42 5TU					
VAT Registration No. 298 3827 04					

Alpha Group   **Customer account code: ALP01**
Alpha House
Warwick   **Delivery note number: 2132**
WR11 5TB

                                         Date: 1 Dec 20XX

Invoice No: 950

Quantity of cases	Product code	Total list price £	Net amount after discount £	VAT £	Gross £
200	A1	2,000	1,800	360	2,160

(b)

Sales daybook					
Date 20XX	Details	Invoice No:	Total £	VAT £	Net £
1 Dec	Alpha Group	950	2,160	360	1,800

(c)

Invoice 189

(d) **(i)**

£594

(ii)

£600

24 SDB

Sales daybook

Date 20XX	Details	Invoice number	Total £	VAT £	Net £	Sales type 1 £	Sales type 2 £
31 Dec	Poonams	105	3,600	600	3,000		3,000
31 Dec	D. Taylor	106	7,680	1,280	6,400	6,400	
31 Dec	Smiths	107	3,840	640	3,200		3,200
	Totals		15,120	2,520	12,600	6,400	6,200

25 MAHINDRA LTD

Sales daybook

Date 20XX	Details	Invoice number	Total £	VAT £	Net £	Sales type 1 £	Sales type 2 £
31 Jan	Square Ltd	3567	1,200	200	1,000	1,000	
31 Jan	Oval & Co	3568	9,600	1,600	8,000		8,000
31 Jan	Diamond Ltd	3569	13,200	2,200	11,000		11,000
31 Jan	Triangle Ltd	3570	7,920	1,320	6,600	6,600	
	Totals		31,920	5,320	26,600	7,600	19,000

26 PAR FOR THE COURSE GOLF SUPPLIES

(a)

Discount type	✓
Prompt payment	
Trade	
Bulk	✓

Feedback: Remember that bulk discount relates to discount given by a supplier for sales orders above a certain quantity.

(b)

	£
Net amount after discounts	2,685.00
VAT @ 20%	537.00
Total	3,222.00

Feedback: Net amount = (300 × £5) + (150 × £7.90) = £2,685

(c)

Menu option	✓
Purchases daybook	
Purchase returns daybook	
Cash book	
Sales daybook	✓
Sales returns daybook	
Discounts allowed daybook	
Discounts received daybook	

Date	Customer code	Customer	General ledger code	Invoice number	Net £	VAT code
13 Aug	EREH094	Erehwon Golf Club	Option 1	2808	2,685.00	Option 2

Option 1	✓
1001 Sales – golf equipment	✓
1002 Sales – golf buggies	
4001 Purchases – golf equipment	
7001 Receivables	

Option 2	✓
V0 – 0%	
V5 – 5%	
V20 – 20%	✓

27 LINKEES TOY MAKERS LTD

(a)

Discount type	✓
Prompt payment	✓
Trade	
Bulk	

(b)

	£
Net amount after discounts	675.00
VAT @ 20%	135.00
Total	810.00

(c)

Menu option	✓
Purchases daybook	
Purchase returns daybook	
Cash book	
Sales daybook	✓
Sales returns daybook	
Discounts allowed daybook	
Discounts received daybook	

Date	Customer code	Customer	General ledger code	Invoice number	Net £	VAT code
17 May	THOM08	Thomas' Toys	Option 1	2808	675.00	Option 2

Option 1	✓
1001 Sales – toys	
1002 Sales – board games	✓
4001 Purchases – Inventory	
7001 Receivables	

Option 2	✓
V0 – 0%	
V5 – 5%	
V20 – 20%	✓
V1 – Exempt	

28 MARTA LTD

(a)

Sales invoice 286

(b)

£4,481.28

(c)

£4,668.00

29 DIAMONDS & RUBIES LTD

<table>
<tr><td colspan="4" style="text-align:center">Stavros
121 Baker St
Newcastle, NE1 7DJ</td></tr>
<tr><td colspan="2">To: Diamonds & Rubies Ltd</td><td colspan="2">Date: 31 Aug 20XX</td></tr>
<tr><td>Date 20XX</td><td>Details</td><td>Transaction amount
£</td><td>Outstanding amount
£</td></tr>
<tr><td>5 Aug</td><td>Invoice 3927</td><td>4,640</td><td>4,640</td></tr>
<tr><td>10 Aug</td><td>Credit note 96</td><td>980</td><td>3,660</td></tr>
<tr><td>21 Aug</td><td>Invoice 3964</td><td>1,560</td><td>5,220</td></tr>
<tr><td>28 Aug</td><td>Credit note 104</td><td>650</td><td>4,570</td></tr>
<tr><td>30 Aug</td><td>Cheque received</td><td>2,100</td><td>2,470</td></tr>
</table>

30 MAX LTD

<table>
<tr><td colspan="4" style="text-align:center">Painting Supplies Ltd
19 Edmund St
Newcastle, NE6 5DJ</td></tr>
<tr><td colspan="2">To: Max Ltd</td><td colspan="2">Date: 28 Feb 20XX</td></tr>
<tr><td>Date 20XX</td><td>Details</td><td>Transaction amount
£</td><td>Outstanding amount
£</td></tr>
<tr><td>5 Feb</td><td>Invoice 4658</td><td>2,560</td><td>2,560</td></tr>
<tr><td>11 Feb</td><td>Invoice 3964</td><td>3,290</td><td>5,850</td></tr>
<tr><td>21 Feb</td><td>Credit note 125</td><td>230</td><td>5,620</td></tr>
<tr><td>23 Feb</td><td>Credit note 139</td><td>560</td><td>5,060</td></tr>
<tr><td>27 Feb</td><td>Cheque received</td><td>1,900</td><td>3,160</td></tr>
</table>

31 BETA BOARDS

<table>
<tr>
<td colspan="4" align="center">**Beta Boards**
3 Victoria Avenue
Troon
KA5 2BD</td>
</tr>
<tr>
<td colspan="2">**To:** Ava Ltd</td>
<td colspan="2" align="right">**Date:** 31 Aug 20XX</td>
</tr>
<tr>
<td>**Date 20XX**</td>
<td>**Details**</td>
<td align="center">**Transaction amount**
£</td>
<td align="center">**Outstanding amount**
£</td>
</tr>
<tr>
<td>10 Aug</td>
<td>Invoice 222</td>
<td align="center">350</td>
<td align="center">350</td>
</tr>
<tr>
<td>12 Aug</td>
<td>Cheque</td>
<td align="center">225</td>
<td align="center">125</td>
</tr>
<tr>
<td>15 Aug</td>
<td>Invoice 305</td>
<td align="center">744</td>
<td align="center">869</td>
</tr>
<tr>
<td>20 Aug</td>
<td>Credit note 194</td>
<td align="center">339</td>
<td align="center">530</td>
</tr>
<tr>
<td>24 Aug</td>
<td>Cheque</td>
<td align="center">530</td>
<td align="center">0</td>
</tr>
</table>

32 BELLA PUMPKIN

(a) – (b)

Bella Pumpkin

Date 20XX	Details	Amount £	Date 20XX	Details	Amount £
12 Dec	Invoice 1001	1,700	21 Dec	Credit note 101	940
21 Dec	Invoice 1004	2,350	29 Dec	Cheque rec'd	2,000
27 Dec	Invoice 1010	470	31 Dec	Balance c/d	1,580
		4,520			**4,520**
20XY 1 Jan	Balance b/d	1,580			

(c)

<table>
<tr>
<td colspan="4" align="center">**Rocky Ricardo**
1 Rocky Way
Middleton, M42 5TU</td>
</tr>
<tr>
<td colspan="2">**To:** Bella Pumpkin</td>
<td colspan="2" align="right">**Date:** 31 Dec 20XX</td>
</tr>
<tr>
<td>**Date 20XX**</td>
<td>**Details**</td>
<td align="center">**Transaction amount**
£</td>
<td align="center">**Outstanding amount**
£</td>
</tr>
<tr>
<td>12 Dec</td>
<td>Invoice 1001</td>
<td align="center">1,700</td>
<td align="center">1,700</td>
</tr>
<tr>
<td>21 Dec</td>
<td>Invoice 1004</td>
<td align="center">2,350</td>
<td align="center">4,050</td>
</tr>
<tr>
<td>21 Dec</td>
<td>Credit note 101</td>
<td align="center">940</td>
<td align="center">3,110</td>
</tr>
<tr>
<td>27 Dec</td>
<td>Invoice 1010</td>
<td align="center">470</td>
<td align="center">3,580</td>
</tr>
<tr>
<td>29 Dec</td>
<td>Cheque</td>
<td align="center">2,000</td>
<td align="center">1,580</td>
</tr>
</table>

33   LAYLA LTD

(a)

Transaction type	Date	Details	Amount £	Action
Balance b/f	1 Aug 20XX		473.87	Allocate full amount – 3671
Invoice 1046	4 Aug 20XX	Goods	1,059.60	Query underpayment
Invoice 1059	9 Aug 20XX	Services	462.20	Query overpayment
Invoice 1068	10 Aug 20XX	Goods	789.48	Allocate full amount – 3684
Invoice 1096	14 Aug 20XX	Goods	662.20	Allocate full amount – 3684

Feedback:

Balance b/f – This amount matches the amount remitted against Invoice 1028. Action is to allocate full amount – in relation to remittance 3671.

Invoice 1046 – The amount remitted of £1,006.62 is £1,059.60 less 5% settlement discount. However, the invoice was settled 12 days after it was raised so the discount should not have been taken. Action is to query underpayment.

Invoice 1059 – The amount remitted of £462.20 is equivalent to the amount of the invoice. However, this was paid within 7 days so qualifies for the settlement discount. Action is to query overpayment.

Invoice 1068 – The amount remitted of £789.48 is equivalent to the amount of the invoice which does not qualify for a settlement discount as paid after 12 days. Action is to allocate full amount – in relation to remittance 3684.

Invoice 1096 – The amount remitted of £629.09 is equivalent to the amount of the invoice less settlement discount which it qualifies for as paid within 10 days of the invoice date. Action is to allocate full amount – in relation to remittance 3684.

(b)

Customer name	Invoice number	Amount before discount £	Amount after prompt payment discount £
Oliver John & Co	387	8,345.60	7,928.32
Excelsior Ltd	395	4,562.40	4,334.28

(c)

Customer name	Prompt payment Discount %	Invoice amount £	Amount paid £	Amount that should have been paid £	Amount outstanding £
Galahad	5	7,529.40	7,093.52	7,152.93	59.41

Feedback: The correct payment is £7,529.40 × 95% = £7,152.93

34 KLOPP & CO

(a)

Transaction type	Date	Details	Amount £	Action
Balance b/f	1 Apr 20XX		752.34	Allocate full amount – 2976
Invoice 354	2 Apr 20XX	Goods	475.61	Allocate full amount – 2976
Invoice 362	9 Apr 20XX	Services	834.25	Query underpayment
Invoice 371	12 Apr 20XX	Services	245.50	Allocate full amount – 2976
Invoice 379	13 Apr 20XX	Goods	1,051.34	Allocate full amount – 3018
Credit note 46	14 Apr 20XX	Correction – 379	178.72	Allocate full amount – 3018
Invoice 383	14 Apr 20XX	Goods	649.23	Allocate full amount – 3018
Invoice 391	19 Apr 20XX	Goods	507.75	Allocate full amount – 3018

Feedback:

Invoice 342 – the invoice made up the opening balance of £752.34. The opening balance is dated 1 April so does not qualify for a settlement discount as the remittance is dated 17 April which is more than the required discount period of 7 days. The full balance of £752.34 has been received. Action is to allocate the full amount – in relation to remittance 2976.

Invoice 354 – the invoice amount is £475.61. The invoice date is 2 April so does not qualify for a settlement discount as the remittance is dated 17 April which is more than the required period of 7 days. The full balance of £475.61 has been received. Action is to allocate the full amount – in relation to remittance 2976.

Invoice 362 – the invoice amount is £834.25 and the invoice is dated 9 April so does not qualify for a settlement discount as the remittance is dated 17 April which is more than the required period of 7 days. The amount received is £800.88 (the settlement discount has been incorrectly deducted). Action is to query the underpayment.

Invoice 371 – the invoice amount is £245.50 and the invoice is dated 12 April so qualifies for a settlement discount as the remittance is dated 17 April which is less than the required period of 7 days. The discounted amount of £235.68 (£245.50 × 96%) has been correctly received. Action is to allocate the full amount – in relation to remittance 2976.

Invoice 379 and Credit Note 46 – The invoice did not qualify for a prompt payment discount. The invoice amount of £1,051.34 less the credit note amount of £178.72 equates to £872.62 which agrees to what was remitted. Action is to allocate the full amount – in relation to remittance 3018.

Invoice 383 – the invoice amount is £649.23 and the invoice is dated 14 April so does not qualify for a settlement discount as the remittance is dated 24 April which is more than the required period of 7 days. The amount of £649.23 has been correctly received. Action is to allocate the full amount – in relation to remittance 3018.

Invoice 391 – the invoice amount is £507.75 and the invoice is dated 19 April so qualifies for a settlement discount as the remittance is dated 24 April which is less than the required period of 7 days. The discounted amount of £487.44 (£507.75 × 96%) has been correctly received. Action is to allocate the full amount – in relation to remittance 3018.

(b)

Reason	✓
The customer has taken a prompt payment discount of 6% that they were not entitled to, on an invoice of £1,958 before the discount.	✓
Henderson & Co have duplicated an invoice in their system for £96.90 plus 20% VAT.	
2 credit notes for £49.71 and £67.77 have been omitted by Henderson & Co.	✓
The customer has paid for £117.48 of goods that they never received.	

Feedback: Item 1 – results in an underpayment of £1,958 × 6% = £117.48. Item 2 – the duplicated invoice amounts to a gross amount of £96.90 × 120% = £116.28. Item 3 – The credit notes amount to £117.48 resulting in a payment less than expected. Item 4 – If the customer paid for goods not received it would result in an overpayment.

PROCESS SUPPLIER TRANSACTIONS

35   NAN NURSING

(a) Has the correct purchase price of the chocolate puddings been charged on the invoice?   N

(b) Has the correct discount been applied?   Y

(c) What would be the VAT amount charged if the invoice was correct?   £18.00

(d) What would be the total amount charged if the invoice was correct?   £108.00

36   PIXIE PAPER

(a) Has the correct product been supplied by Pixie Paper?   Y

(b) Has the correct net price been calculated?   N

(c) Has the total invoice price been calculated correctly?   N

(d) What would be the VAT amount charged if the invoice was correct?   £90.00

(e) What would be the total amount charged if the invoice was correct?   £540.00

Feedback re (b) – the trade discount of 10% should have been deducted so that the net price was £450. VAT @ 20% on the net price of £450 is then calculated as £90.00.

37   PAINTS R US

(a) Has the correct product been supplied?   Y

(b) Has the correct net price been calculated?   Y

(c) Has the total invoice price been calculated correctly?   N

(d) What would be the VAT amount charged if the invoice was correct?   £32.00

(e) What would be the total amount charged if the invoice was correct?   £192.00

38   MT MOTORS

(a)   **B**   £400.00

	£
List price	500
Less: Trade discount (20% × £500)	(100)
	———
Purchases	400
	———

(b)   **B**   £80.00

	£
List price	500.00
Less: Trade discount	(100.00)
	———
Net purchases	400.00
VAT @ 20%	80.00
	———
	480.00
	———

(c)   **A**   It is issued to a supplier to request supply of goods from them on terms specified within the order.

39   ECHO LTD

(a)

Has the correct discount been applied?	N
How much should the trade discount amount be?	£100
What would be the VAT amount charged if the invoice was correct?	£180

(b)

Daybook: Purchase daybook					
Date 20XX	Details	Invoice No:	Total £	VAT £	Net £
10 Dec	Messi Brothers	**1365**	2,250	375	1,875

40   NORTH RIPONIA RAILWAY

(a)

Daybook	✓
Sales daybook	
Purchases daybook	
Cashbook	
Purchase returns daybook	✓
Sales returns daybook	
Discounts allowed daybook	

(b)

Date 20XX	Supplier	Credit note number	Net £	VAT £	Total £
17 May	Narrow Gauge Ltd	CN869	317.60	63.52	381.12
26 June	Island of Sodor plc	CN0289	84.00	16.80	100.80
8 Aug	Topham Hatt & Co	421·	98.50	19.70	118.20
13 Sep	Flying Kipper Ltd	C980	206.00	41.20	247.20
14 Oct	Gamel's Train Repairs	CN483	476.50	95.30	571.80
		Totals	1,182.60	236.52	1,419.12

(c)

Discrepancy	✓
Date of invoice	
Product type	
Quantity of product	
Unit price	✓
VAT rate	
Total	✓

Feedback: The total does not cast correctly.

41 MARCIN & CO

(a)

Daybook	✓
Sales daybook	
Purchases daybook	✓
Cashbook	
Purchase returns daybook	
Sales returns daybook	
Discounts allowed daybook	

(b)

Date 20XX	Supplier	Invoice number	Net £	VAT £	Total £
8 Mar	Norris Ltd	3897	1,010.00	202.00	1,212.00
10 Mar	Sam Jones	0187	878.40	175.68	1,054.08
11 Mar	James & Sarah Ltd	402929	463.80	92.76	556.56
11 Mar	Trevor Dylis Ltd	73910	1,329.10	265.82	1,594.92
14 Mar	Henry's Office Supplies	7208	584.00	116.80	700.80
		Totals	4,265.30	853.06	5,118.36

(c)

Discrepancy	✓
Prompt payment discount value	
VAT	✓
Invoice number	✓
Total	

Feedback: The VAT should be £2.70 calculated as £135 × 2% or £13.50 × 20%

42   FREDDIE LTD

Purchases daybook

Date 20XX	Details	Invoice number	Total £	VAT £	Net £	Product 14211 £	Product 14212 £
31 July	Box Ltd	2177	960	160	800	800	
31 July	Shrew Ltd	2175	14,400	2,400	12,000	12,000	
31 July	Novot & Co	2176	4,800	800	4,000		4,000
	Totals		20,160	3,360	16,800	12,800	4,000

43   ALPHA LTD

(a)

Purchase return £900

(b)

Invoice 486

(c)

£8,580.00

44   MAXIMUS LTD

(a)

Alpha Ltd
121 Baker St
Newcastle, NE1 7DJ
REMITTANCE ADVICE

To: Maximus Ltd 20XX   **Date:** 31 Aug

Please find attached our cheque in payment of the following amounts.

Invoice number	Credit note number	Amount £
864		6,386
	252	964
	258	1,218
	Total amount paid	4,204

(b)

A remittance note is for our records only   F

A remittance note is sent to a supplier to advise them of the amount being paid   T

45   HOLLY LTD

(a)

Purchase return 286

(b)

£928.80

(c)

£172.00

(d)

£1,032.00

46   EP MANUFACTURERS

(a)

Cheque for £1,200

(b)

Invoice 488

(c)

£4,850.00

47   STANNY LTD

(a)

	Ringo Rings	
	37 Parker Lane	
	Stoke SK1 0KE	

REMITTANCE ADVICE

To: Stanny Ltd   **Date:** 31 Mar 20XX

Please find attached our cheque in payment of the following amounts.

Invoice number	Credit note number	Amount £
694		2,300
658		3,640
	198	650
	154	1,250
	Total amount paid	**4,040**

(b)

A remittance note is for our and the suppliers records   T

A remittance note is sent by a supplier confirming amounts received from them   F

48   TOYWORLD

(a)

Cheque for £500

Picklist: Invoice 207, Invoice 310, Invoice 504, Invoice 505, Cheque for £3,400, Cheque for £500

(b)

Invoice 505

Picklist: Invoice 207, Invoice 310, Invoice 504, Invoice 505, Cheque for £3,400, Cheque for £500

(c)

£4,000

49   HENRY HOUSE

(a)

Henry House

22 Nursery Road

Keighley, BD22 7BD

REMITTANCE ADVICE

To: Abbies Party

Date: 31 August 20XX

Please find attached our cheque in payment of the following amounts.

Invoice number	Credit note number	Amount £
242		220
	27	82
Total amount paid		138

(b)

    D   The remittance advice note will be sent to the supplier to advise them of the amount being paid.

50 GREY GARAGES

Remittance advice			
To: Mulberry Motors			
From: Grey Garages			
Payment method: BACS		**Date of payment:** 25 July	

Items outstanding			**Tick if included in payment**
Date 20XX	**Details**	**Amount** £	
23-Jun	Invoice 213	740	✓
06-Jul	Credit note 14	120	✓
13-Jul	Invoice 216	620	✓
19-Jul	Invoice 257	870	
	Total amount paid		£1,240

51 ERRICO

Supplier	£	Date by which the payment should be received by the supplier
Giacomo	67.51	11 June 20XX
Gaetani	39.33	9 June 20XX

52 LEVIN & CO

(a)

Supplier	£	Date by which the payment should be received by the supplier
Bridge Brothers	110.25	23rd October
Mitchells	128.79	24th October

(b)

Xcess Stock Unit 7 Windy Industrial Estate Irvine, KA6 8HU To: Levin & Co Date: 31 Dec 20XX			Not to be paid
Date 20XX	Details	Transaction amount £	
12 Dec	Invoice 1001	1,700	
13 Dec	Invoice 1003	1,500	✓
21 Dec	Invoice 1004	2,350	
21 Dec	Credit note 101	940	
22 Dec	Invoice 1005	450	✓
27 Dec	Invoice 1010	470	
28 Dec	Credit note 102	50	✓

(c)

£3,580

(d)

£1,516

53   KINSHASA LTD

(a)

Supplier name	Invoice amount £	Invoice date 20XX	Amount to be paid £	Date by which supplier should receive payment
Kennack & Co	756.90	9 Jan	756.90	8 February
Butterworth & Sons	1,317.83	11 Jan	1,317.83	10 February
Jermyn Ltd	847.60	10 Jan	805.22	17 January

Feedback: Only Jermyn Ltd should be paid early as the others do not offer discounts of 5% or more. The payment will be £847.60 × 95% = £805.22.

(b)

Transactions	✓
Opening balance	✓
Invoice 287	✓
Invoice 294	
Invoice 304	✓
Invoice 307	
Invoice 307	
Credit note 045	
Invoice 342	

Feedback: The payment of £5,296 = £639 + £1,204 + £3,453

(c)

Type of error	✓
Underpayment	
Overpayment	
Missing transactions	
Duplicate transaction	✓
Timing difference	

Feedback: Invoice 307 is recorded twice.

54   FARFIELD LTD

(a)

Supplier name	Invoice amount £	Invoice date 20XX	Amount to be paid £	Date by which supplier should receive payment
Archer Joinery	1,340.00	25 Aug	1,340.00	30 September
Sankey Electrical	4,372.80	26 Aug	4,263.48	9 September
Pannal Construction	3,720.00	26 Aug	3,608.40	5 September

(b)

Transactions	✓
Opening balance	✓
Invoice 308	
Invoice 314	✓
Credit note 048	✓
Invoice 326	
Invoice 338	
Invoice 343	

Feedback: the cheque for £1,605 = £1,160 + £1,342 − £897

(c)

Type of error	✓
Underpayment	
Timing difference	✓
Overpayment	
Missing transactions	
Duplicate transaction	

Feedback: The difference of £896 relates to CHQ 0786 which was presumably sent by Farfield Ltd before the month end but received by Kelham builders on 2 October.

PROCESS RECEIPTS AND PAYMENTS

55   ABC LTD

(a)   Cash book – Credit side

Details	Cash	Bank	VAT	Payables	Cash purchases	Repairs and renewals
Balance b/f						
S. Lampard	216		36		180	
S. Bobbins	264		44		220	
Penny Rhodes	530				530	
Henley's Ltd		4,925		4,925		
Epic Equipment Maintenance		480	80			400
Total	**1,010**	**5,405**	**160**	**4,925**	**930**	**400**

(b) **Cash book – Debit side**

Details	Cash	Bank	Receivables
Balance b/f	1,550	7,425	
D Davies		851	851
E Denholm		450	450
Total	**1,550**	**8,726**	**1,301**

(c) **Using your answers to (a) and (b) above calculate the cash balance.**

£540

(d) **Using your answers to (a) and (b) above calculate the bank balance.**

£3,321

(e) **Debit**

56 BEDS

(a) **Cash book – Credit side**

Details	Cash	Bank	VAT	Payables	Cash purchases	Repairs and renewals
Balance b/f						
A. Blighty Ltd	708		118		590	
R Bromby	228		38		190	
Roxy Bland	230				230	
Burgess Ltd		2,400		2,400		
Fast Equipment Repairs		96	16			80
Total	**1,166**	**2,496**	**172**	**2,400**	**1,010**	**80**

(b) **Cash book – Debit side**

Details	Cash	Bank	Receivables
Balance b/f	1,175	3,825	
A Barnett		698	698
H Connelly		250	250
Total	**1,175**	**4,773**	**948**

(c) **Using your answers to (a) and (b) above calculate the cash balance.**

£9

(d) **Using your answers to (a) and (b) above calculate the bank balance.**

£2,277

(e) **Will the bank balance calculated in (d) above be a debit or credit balance?**

Debit

57   JO'S

(a)   Cash book – credit side

Details	Cash	Bank	VAT	Payables	Cash purchases	Stationery expenses
Bal b/f		19,546				
T. Hunkin Ltd	48		8		40	
Victoria Green	96		16		80	
B. Head Ltd	455				455	
Smiths Ltd		4,250		4,250		
Arrow Valley Stationers		120	20			100
Total	599	23,916	44	4,250	575	100

(b)   Cash book – debit side

Details	Cash	Bank	Receivables
Balance b/f	986		
J Drummond		623	623
N Atkinson		425	425
Total	986	1,048	1,048

(c)   Using your answers to (a) and (b) above calculate the cash balance.

£387

(d)   Using your answers to (a) and (b) above calculate the bank balance.

£22,868

(e)   Will the bank balance calculated in (d) above be a debit or a credit balance?

Credit

58   **LAGOS**

(a)   **Cash book – Credit side**

Details	Cash	Bank	VAT	Payables	Cash purchases	Motor expenses
Balance b/f		11,450				
J Pumpkin	960		160		800	
B Row	240		40		200	
Lemon Ltd		100		100		
Remo Motor		240	40			200
Fencer		600		600		
Total	1,200	12,390	240	700	1,000	200

(b)   **Cash book – Debit side**

Details	Cash	Bank	Receivables
Balance b/f	1,850		
Jeff Jolly		127	127
Dolly Darton		310	310
Total	1,850	437	437

(c)

£650

(d)

£11,953

(e)

Credit

59 MANGROVE

Date 20XX	Details	Cash £	Bank £	VAT £	Cash purchases	Payables £
25 May	K Quick	334.80		55.80	279.00	
26 May	Whiles Ltd		1,374.00			1,374.00
27 May	Sasha and Co	418.80		69.80	349.00	

Feedback: K Quick VAT = £279.00 × 20% = £55.80. No VAT is recorded for Whiles Ltd as this payment settles a trade payable. The VAT would have been recorded when the original invoice was recorded in the purchases daybook. Sasha and Co VAT = £418.80 × 20/120 = £69.80.

60 SWAMP

(a)

Date 20XX	Details	Cash £	Bank £	VAT £	Cash sales	Receiv- ables
23 Aug	Bal b/f	1,089.70	8,539.43			
23 Aug	Bennett Ltd		2,924.40			2,924.40
25 Aug	J Smith	586.56		97.76	488.80	
		1,676.26	11,463.83			

(b)

£	862.78

Feedback: No VAT is shown relating to the credit customer as it is dealt with in the sales daybook. The credit side of the cash book shows the total cash payments were £813.48.

61 QUEEN VIC

(a)

Amount in petty cash box	**£141.00**
Balance on petty cash account	**£145.00**
Difference	**£4.00**

(b)

Petty cash reimbursement	
Date: 31.07.20XX	
Amount required to restore the cash in the petty cash box.	**£122.75**

62 THE ARCHES

(a) – (b)

Petty cash book

Debit side		Credit side					
Details	Amount £	Details	Amount £	VAT £	Postage £	Travel £	Stationery £
Balance b/f	200.00	Mick's Motors	20.00			20.00	
		Stamps	19.00		19.00		
		Office Essentials	26.40	4.40			22.00
		Balance c/d	134.60				
	200.00		**200.00**	**4.40**	**19.00**	**20.00**	**22.00**

63 RAINBOW

(a) – (b)

Petty cash book

Debit side		Credit side					
Details	Amount £	Details	Amount £	VAT £	Postage £	Travel £	Stationery £
Balance b/f	100.00	Colin's Cabs	28.00			28.00	
		Post Office	18.00		18.00		
		ABC Stationery	38.40	6.40			32.00
		Balance c/d	15.60				
	100.00		**100.00**	**6.40**	**18.00**	**28.00**	**32.00**

64   SOOTY AND SWEEP

(a)

Amount in petty cash box	**£127.40**
Balance on petty cash account	**£135.00**
Difference	**£7.60**

(b)

Petty cash reimbursement	
Date: 31.07.20XX	
Amount required to restore the cash in the petty cash box.	**£245.00**

65   PEREZ

(a) – (b)

Petty cash book

Debit side		Credit side					
Details	**Amount £**	**Details**	**Amount £**	**VAT £**	**Postage £**	**Travel £**	**Stationery £**
Balance b/f	225.00	Ace Taxis	26.00			26.00	
		Kate's Couriers	27.00		27.00		
		Smiths Stationery	45.60	7.60			38.00
		Balance c/d	126.40				
	225.00		225.00	7.60	27.00	26.00	38.00

66   TOMAS'S TILES

(a)

Amount in petty cash box	**£162.12**
Balance on petty cash account	**£165.52**
Difference	**£3.40**

(b)

Petty cash reimbursement	
Date: 30.04.20XX	
Amount required to restore the cash in the petty cash box.	**£224.12**

67   ROCKY RILEY

(a) – (b)

Petty cash book

Debit side		Credit side					
Details	Amount £	Details	Amount £	VAT £	Postage £	Travel £	Stationery £
Balance b/f	175.00	Kath's Kars	32.00			32.00	
		Stamps	25.00		25.00		
		Pauline's Pens	24.00	4.00			20.00
		Balance c/d	94.00				
	175.00		175.00	**4.00**	**25.00**	**32.00**	**20.00**

68   MHAIRI MOTORS

(a)

Amount in petty cash box	**£99.80**
Balance on petty cash account	**£110.00**
Difference	**£10.20**

(b)

Petty cash reimbursement	
Date: 31.07.20XX	
Amount required to restore the cash in the petty cash box.	**£191.50**

69   DAINTY DESIGNS

(a)

VAT £	Net £
5.20	26.00

(b)

£91.66

(c)

Details	Amount £	Debit ✓	Credit ✓
Cash from bank	237.70	✓	

(d)

Details	Amount £	Debit ✓	Credit ✓
Balance c/d	280.00		✓

(e)

Petty cash voucher	Total £	VAT £	Net £
222	32.40	5.40	27.00
223	12.00	2.00	10.00

70   RIVERA MOTORING

(a)

VAT £	Net £
3.60	18.00

(b)

£33.50

(c)

Details	Amount £	Debit ✓	Credit ✓
Cash from bank	183.45	✓	

(d)

Details	Amount £	Debit ✓	Credit ✓
Balance c/d	215.00		✓

(e)

Petty cash voucher	Total £	VAT £	Net £
120	20.00	0	20.00
121	19.20	3.20	16.00

71 WHILES LTD

(a)

Details	Amount £	Debit ✓	Credit ✓
See below	302.17	✓	

Details	✓
Balance brought down	
Bank	✓
Sales	
Cash	

Feedback: In an imprest system the amounts paid from petty cash are then transferred from the bank account in order to maintain the float.

(b)

	✓
A missing petty cash voucher for £16.67 excluding VAT	✓
Cash of £20 has been stolen from petty cash	
A petty cash voucher for £20 has yet to be recorded in the petty cash book	
A petty cash transaction of £64.20 was incorrectly recorded in the petty cash book as £84.20	✓

Feedback: The missing petty cash voucher would be £16.67 × 120% = £20 which is the difference between the vouchers and petty cash book totals. Stolen cash would not affect the vouchers recording expenditure or the petty cash book itself. If the petty cash voucher had not been recorded then the vouchers would exceed the petty cash book total. This error of £20 results in the petty cash book expenditure exceeding the amount of the vouchers.

(c)

£	64.00

Feedback: The VAT would be recognised separately in the VAT column of the petty cash book. The net expenditure on cleaning is (£48 × 100/120) + £24 = £64.

72   BAKER LTD

Date 20XX	Details	Cash £	VAT £	Cleaning £	Travel £	Food/drink £	Stationery £
30 Nov	Bal b/f	89.40	14.90	14.50	36.00	–	12.00
30 Nov	Window cleaning	28.50	4.75	23.75			
30 Nov	A4 binders	43.20	7.20				36.00

73   BUTCHER LTD

(a)   **Set up the recurring entry in the digital bookkeeping system.**

Transaction type	General ledger code	Start date 20XX	End date 20XX	Frequency	Net amount £	VAT code
Bank	Option 1	Option 2	Option 3	Monthly	25.00	Option 4

Option 1	✓
7100 – Insurance	
1100 – Van non-current assets	
2000 – Bank	
7400 – Motor lease costs	✓

Option 2	✓
5 Jun 20XX	
5 May 20XX	✓
5 Nov 20XX	
5 Dec 20XX	

Option 3	✓
5 Jun 20XX	
5 May 20XX	
5 Nov 20XX	
5 Dec 20XX	✓

Option 4	✓
V0 – 0%	
V1 – Exempt	
V20 – 20%	✓
V5 – 5%	

(b)   **Identify ONE effect of processing the recurring entry.**

Effect	✓
The standing order will be automatically set up to pay for the lease costs	
Entries will be posted to all relevant general ledger accounts	✓
Entries will be posted to the receivables ledger and all relevant general ledger accounts	

74   CHANDLER LTD

(a)

Information	✓
The number of recurring transactions	
The frequency of the recurring transactions	
The total value of all recurring transactions	✓
The VAT rate	

(b)

Transaction type	General ledger code	Start date 20XX	End date 20XX	Frequency	Net amount £	VAT code
Bank	Option 1	Option 2	Option 3	Monthly	400	Option 4

Option 1	✓
7560 – Rent expense	
1040 – Office equipment	
2000 – Bank	
4000 – Maintenance services	✓

Option 2	✓
10 Apr 20XX	
10 May 20XX	
10 Feb 20XX	✓
10 Jul 20XX	

Option 3	✓
10 Apr 20XX	
10 May 20XX	
10 Feb 20XX	
10 Jul 20XX	✓

Option 4	✓
V0 – 0%	
V1 – Exempt	
V20 – 20%	✓
V5 – 5%	

PROCESS TRANSACTIONS INTO LEDGER ACCOUNTS

75   LADY LTD

General ledger

Payables ledger control account

	£		£
		1 Dec Balance b/d	5,103.90
		18 Dec Purchases & Vat	**903.23**

VAT account

	£		£
		1 Dec Balance b/d	526.90
18 Dec PLCA	**150.53**		

Purchases account

	£		£
1 Dec Balance b/d	22,379.52		
18 Dec PLCA	**752.70**		

Subsidiary ledger

M Brown

	£		£
		1 Dec Balance b/d	68.50
		1 Dec PDB	**300.00**

H Madden

	£		£
		1 Dec Balance b/d	286.97
		5 Dec PDB	**183.55**

L Singh

	£		£
		1 Dec Balance b/d	125.89
		7 Dec PDB	**132.60**

A Stevens

	£		£
		1 Dec Balance b/d	12.36
		10 Dec PDB	**90.00**

N Shema

	£		£
		1 Dec Balance b/d	168.70
		18 Dec PDB	**197.08**

76 SATO LTD

(a)

Account name	Amount £	Debit ✓	Credit ✓
Peak & Co	6,240		✓
Max Ltd	12,720		✓
McIntyre Wholesale	5,760		✓
Pigmy Ltd	3,744		✓

(b)

Account name	Amount £	Debit ✓	Credit ✓
Purchases	23,720	✓	
VAT	4,744	✓	
Payables ledger control	28,464		✓

77 SPARKY LTD

(a)   Receivables ledger

Account name	Amount £	Debit ✓	Credit ✓
Clarkson Ltd	1,680		✓
Kyle & Co	720		✓

(b) General ledger

Account name	Amount £	Debit ✓	Credit ✓
Receivables ledger control account	2,400		✓
Sales returns	2,000	✓	
VAT	400	✓	

78 LOUIS LTD

(a)

Account name	Amount £	Debit ✓	Credit ✓
Sheep & Co	3,840	✓	
Cow Ltd	11,760	✓	
Chicken & Partners	6,720	✓	
Pig Ltd	14,496	✓	

(b)

Account name	Amount £	Debit ✓	Credit ✓
Receivables ledger control	36,816	✓	
VAT	6,136		✓
Sales	30,680		✓

79 TANAKA

(a) Payables ledger

Account name	Amount £	Debit ✓	Credit ✓
May Ltd	1,920	✓	
Hammond & Co	1,200	✓	

(b) General ledger

Account name	Amount £	Debit ✓	Credit ✓
Payables ledger control account	3,120	✓	
Purchase returns	2,600		✓
VAT	520		✓

80 ALEX

(a)

Account name	Amount £	Debit ✓	Credit ✓
Lou and Phil's	5,040	✓	
Eddie and Co	10,560	✓	
Noah's Arc	2,880	✓	
Alex and Freddie	720	✓	

(b)

Account name	Amount £	Debit ✓	Credit ✓
Sales	16,000		✓
VAT	3,200		✓
Receivables ledger control	19,200	✓	

81 JESSICA & CO

(a) **Payables ledger**

Account name	Amount £	Debit ✓	Credit ✓
Iona Ltd	1,680	✓	
Matilda Ltd	4,320	✓	

(b) **General ledger**

Account name	Amount £	Debit ✓	Credit ✓
Payables ledger control account	6,000	✓	
Purchases returns	5,000		✓
VAT	1,000		✓

82 HORSEY REACH

(a)

Account name	Amount £	Debit ✓	Credit ✓
Receivables ledger control	226.80		✓
VAT	37.80	✓	
Discounts allowed	189.00	✓	

(b)

Account name	Amount £	Debit ✓	Credit ✓
Ashleigh Buildings	36.00		✓
143 WGT	54.00		✓
McDuff McGregor	43.20		✓
Cameron Travel	93.60		✓

83 BUTTERFLY BEES

(a)

Account name	Amount £	Debit ✓	Credit ✓
Discounts received	356.00		✓
VAT	71.20		✓
Payables ledger control	427.20	✓	

(b)

Account name	Amount £	Debit ✓	Credit ✓
Bella Bumps	24.00	✓	

84 OLIVIA ROSE BRIDAL SUPPLIES

(a)

Account name	Amount £	Debit ✓	Credit ✓
Discounts allowed	189.00	✓	
VAT	37.80	✓	
Receivables ledger control	226.80		✓

(b)

Account name	Amount £	Debit ✓	Credit ✓
Bridezilla	54.00		✓

85 GIRONDE TRADING

(a)

Account name	Amount £	Debit ✓	Credit ✓
Discounts allowed	410.00	✓	
VAT	82.00	✓	
Receivables ledger control	492.00		✓

(b)

Account name	Amount £	Debit ✓	Credit ✓
Woody Woodburn	78.00		✓

86 ROXY CAKE DESIGNS

(a)

Account name	Amount £	Debit ✓	Credit ✓
Discounts allowed	318.00	✓	
VAT	63.60	✓	
Receivables ledger control	381.60		✓

(b)

Account name	Amount £	Debit ✓	Credit ✓
Percy Tran	33.60		✓

87   CANTAL SUPPLIES

(a)

Account name	Amount £	Debit/Credit
Purchases returns	4,580.00	Credit
VAT	916.00	Credit
Payables ledger control	5,496.00	Debit

(b)

Account name	Amount £	Debit/Credit
Sales returns	2,501.00	Debit
VAT	500.20	Debit
Receivables ledger control	3,001.20	Credit

88   NC CLEANING SUPPLIES

(a)

Account name	Amount £	Debit/Credit
Payables ledger control	318.00	Debit
VAT	53.00	Credit
Purchases returns	265.00	Credit

(b)

Account name	Amount £	Debit/Credit
Sales returns	150.00	Debit
VAT	30.00	Debit
Receivables ledger control	180.00	Credit

89   CHUGGER LTD

(a)   **General ledger**

Account name	Amount £	Debit ✓	Credit ✓
Stationery expense	80	✓	
Repairs	200	✓	
VAT	56	✓	

(b)   **Receivables ledger**

Account name	Amount £	Debit ✓	Credit ✓
BBG Ltd	7,200		✓
EFG Ltd	5,000		✓

(c)   **General ledger**

Account name	Amount £	Debit ✓	Credit ✓
Receivables ledger control	12,200		✓

90   ITALIAN STALLIONS

(a)   **General ledger**

Account name	Amount £	Debit ✓	Credit ✓
Office supplies	80	✓	
Repairs	160	✓	
VAT	48	✓	

(b)   **Receivables ledger**

Account name	Amount £	Debit ✓	Credit ✓
AAG Ltd	4,000		✓
HLG Ltd	3,000		✓

(c)   **General ledger**

Account name	Amount £	Debit ✓	Credit ✓
Receivables ledger control	7,000		✓

91   FELA'S FISH

(a)   **Receivables ledger**

Account name	Amount £	Debit ✔	Credit ✔
K and D Ltd	8,200		✔

(b)   **General ledger**

Account name	Amount £	Debit ✔	Credit ✔
Receivables ledger control	8,200		✔

(c)   **General ledger**

Account name	Amount £	Debit ✔	Credit ✔
Stationery	100	✔	
VAT	20	✔	
Postage	800	✔	

92   HICKORY HOUSE

General ledger

Account name	Amount £	Debit ✔	Credit ✔
VAT	6.80	✔	
Postage	15.00	✔	
Motor expenses	12.40	✔	
Office expenses	21.60	✔	
Bank	90		✔

93   MESSI & CO

General ledger

Account name	Amount £	Debit ✔	Credit ✔
VAT	7.25	✔	
Postage	4.50	✔	
Motor expenses	8.00	✔	
Office expenses	28.28	✔	
Petty cash control	48.03		✔

91   FELA'S FISH

94 STAVROS

General ledger

Account name	Amount £	Debit ✓	Credit ✓
VAT	18.86	✓	
Postage	16.00	✓	
Business travel	30.80	✓	
Sundry expenses	63.50	✓	
Bank	110.00		✓

95 YUMMY CUPCAKES

General ledger

Account name	Amount £	Debit ✓	Credit ✓
VAT	11.07	✓	
Sundry expenses	10.00	✓	
Business travel	45.37	✓	
Postage	4.00	✓	
Petty cash control	70.44		✓

96 OOH LA!

General ledger

Account name	Amount £	Debit ✓	Credit ✓
VAT	15.21	✓	
Postage	36.30	✓	
Sundry expenses	35.05	✓	
Motor expenses	17.00	✓	
Bank	70.00		✓

97 LJ INTERIORS

Account name	Amount £	Debit ✓	Credit ✓
VAT	64.00	✓	
Stationery	320.00	✓	
Postage	32.00	✓	
Charitable donations	150.00	✓	

98 KAZ KARATE CLUB

Account name	Amount £	Debit ✓	Credit ✓
VAT	31.00	✓	
Motor expenses	155.00	✓	
Postage	20.00	✓	
Insurance	180.00	✓	

99 JACINTA INTERIOR DESIGN

(a)

Petty cash reimbursement	
Week 22	
Amount required to restore the cash in the petty cash box.	**£243.90**

	£
Stationery	42.30
Travelling cost	76.50
Refreshments	38.70
Sundry payables (£72.00 × (120/100)	86.40
	243.90 to restore to £300

(b)

A   Dr Petty cash   Cr Bank

100 MARTHA

(a)

VAT £	Net £
10.00	50.00

(b)

£62.40

(c)

Details	Amount £	Debit ✓	Credit ✓
Cash from bank	117.36	✓	

(d)

Details	Amount £	Debit ✓	Credit ✓
Balance c/d	150.00		✓

(e)

Petty cash receipt	Analysis column	Amount £
Newark Printers	Office expenses	14.50
ERJ Motor Supplies	Motor expenses	32.00
Co-pop	Cleaning expenses	5.00

101 ROLAND

(a)

Account name	Amount £	Debit ✓	Credit ✓
Receivables ledger control	123.60		✓
VAT	20.60	✓	
Discounts allowed	103.00	✓	

(b)

Account name	Amount £	Debit ✓	Credit ✓
Aldo & Co	24.00		✓
Hopley Brothers	36.00		✓
Fernando's	25.20		✓
Richmond Travel	38.40		✓

102 ROGER

(a) **Receivables ledger**

Account name	Amount £	Debit ✓	Credit ✓
TUV Ltd	4,000		✓

(b) **General ledger**

Account name	Amount £	Debit ✓	Credit ✓
Receivables ledger control	4,000		✓

(c)   **General ledger**

Account name	Amount £	Debit ✓	Credit ✓
Entertainment	160	✓	
VAT	32	✓	
Insurance	240	✓	

103   SAMIA & CO

(a)

Account name	Amount £	Debit ✓	Credit ✓
Cash purchases	4,345.70	✓	
VAT	869.14	✓	
Payables ledger control account	8,671.46	✓	

Feedback: The full journal is

Dr Input VAT £869.14

Dr Purchases £4,345.70

Dr Payables £8,671.46

Cr Cash £3,574.70

Cr Bank £10,311.60

(b)

Daybook	Debit ✓	Credit ✓	Payables ledger ✓	Receivables ledger ✓
Purchases		✓	✓	
Discounts allowed		✓		✓

Feedback: Credit purchases (from the purchases daybook) are credited to payables. Discounts allowed are given to customers and reduce (credit) the receivables balance.

104   S WILLIAMS LTD

(a)

Account name	Amount £	Debit ✓	Credit ✓
Cash sales	2,045.60		✓
VAT	2,013.10		✓
Receivables ledger control account	8,019.90		✓

(b)

Daybook	Debit ✓	Credit ✓	Payables ledger ✓	Receivables ledger ✓
Sales	✓			✓
Discounts received	✓		✓	

Feedback: The sales day book records credit sales, this will impact the receivables ledger by recognising a balance (an asset) due from the receivable on the debit side.

105   BROOKLYN BOATS

(a) – (c)

Electricity

Date 20XX	Details	Amount £	Date 20XX	Details	Amount £
01 Dec	Balance b/f	870	31 Dec	Balance c/d	1,220
12 Dec	Bank	350			
	Total	1,220		Total	1,220
		1,220			

Discounts received

Date 20XX	Details	Amount £	Date 20XX	Details	Amount £
31 Dec	Balance c/d	600	1 Dec	Balance b/f	500
			15 Dec	Payables Ledger control	100
	Total	600		Total	600
			1 Jan	Balance b/d	600

106 WIGGLE POGGLE LTD

(a) – (c)

Discount allowed

Date 20XX	Details	Amount £	Date 20XX	Details	Amount £
01 July	Balance b/f	1,560	31 July	Balance c/d	2,160
14 July	Receivables ledger control account	480			
16 July	Receivables ledger control account	120			
	Total	2,160		**Total**	2,160
1 Aug	Balance b/d	2,160			

Interest income

Date 20XX	Details	Amount £	Date 20XX	Details	Amount £
31 July	Balance c/d	400	01 July	Balance b/f	320
			28 July	Bank	80
	Total	400		**Total**	400
			1 Aug	Balance b/d	400

107 PARDE CURTAINS

(a) – (c)

Electricity expense

Date 20XX	Details	Amount £	Date 20XX	Details	Amount £
01 Jan	Bal b/f	200	31 Jan	Balance c/d	450
22 Jan	Bank	250			
	Total	450		**Total**	450
1 Feb	Balance b/d	450			

Rental income

Date 20XX	Details	Amount £	Date 20XX	Details	Amount £
31 Jan	Balance c/d	1,000	01 Jan	Balance b/f	400
			28 Jan	Bank	600
	Total	1,000		**Total**	1,000
			1 Feb	Balance b/d	1,000

108 BALANCES 1

Account name	Balance c/d at 31 December £	Debit/Credit	Total shown in both the debit and credit columns £
Capital	6,000	Debit	6,000
Fixtures and Fittings	19,800	Credit	21,000
Loan	23,230	Debit	24,880
Drawings	2,450	Credit	2,450

109 BALANCES 2

Account name	Balance c/d at 31 March £	Debit/Credit	Total shown in both the debit and credit columns £
Capital	15,000	Debit	15,000
Plant and Machinery	8,950	Credit	9,750
Loan	14,180	Debit	15,200
Drawings	4,220	Credit	4,220

110 BALANCES 3

(a)

Account	Amount £	Debit ✓	Credit ✓
AD014	1,505		✓
AD019	3,174	✓	
AD036	21		✓

Feedback:

AD014

Date 20XX	Details	Amount £	Date 20XX	Details	Amount £
21 Dec	Bank	465	14 Dec	Cash	947
28 Dec	Bank	1,987			
				Bal c/d	1,505
		2,452			2,452

AD019

Date 20XX	Details	Amount £	Date 20XX	Details	Amount £
19 Dec	Cash	136	3 Dec	Bank	948
			12 Dec	Cash	2,362
	Bal c/d	3,174			
		3,310			3,310

AD036

Date 20XX	Details	Amount £	Date 20XX	Details	Amount £
7 Dec	Cash	754	3 Dec	Bank	856
18 Dec	Bank	429	27 Dec	Cash	306
				Bal c/d	21
		1,183			1,183

(b) **Receivables**

Date	Details	Amount £	Date	Details	Amount £
1 Dec	Balance brought down	9,864	17 Dec	Cash	7,493
21 Dec	Sales	4,928	31 Dec	Balance carried down	7,299
		14,792		Total	14,792
1 Jan	Balance brought down	7,299			

Section 3

MOCK ASSESSMENT QUESTIONS

You have **1 hour and 30 minutes** to complete this practice assessment.

This assessment contains **11 tasks** and you should attempt to complete **every** task.

- Each task is independent. You will not need to refer to your answers to previous tasks.

- The total number of marks for this assessment is 100.

- Read every task carefully to make sure you understand what is required.

- Where the date is relevant, it is given in the task data.

- Both minus signs and brackets can be used to indicate negative numbers **unless** task instructions state otherwise.

- You must use a full stop to indicate a decimal point. For example, write 100.57 **not** 100,57 or 10057.

- You may use a comma to indicate a number in the thousands, but you don't have to. For example, 10000 and 10,000 are both acceptable.

- Mathematical rounding should be applied where appropriate.

Scenario

- The tasks in this assessment are set in different business situations where the following apply:

- Businesses use a variety of bookkeeping systems.

- Double entry takes place in the general ledger.

- The VAT rate is 20%.

TASK 1 (10 MARKS)

This task is about manual and digital bookkeeping systems.

(a)   Which document or report would be used for each of the purposes below?

	Document or report
To identify which specific invoices are being paid off when sending payment	
To issue a refund or to write off an amount owed following a return of goods	
To show the detail of the goods sold and total price	
To show details of the amounts owed from each customer	

Picklist: Credit note, remittance, receivables ledger, sales invoice

(4 marks)

Product codes for specific toys sold consist of a sequentially numbered system based on the name of the product, sorted alphabetically. This is followed by the first two letters of the product type. The first three products in the warehouse are shown below, with the first one filled in.

(b)   Identify the correct product codes for the items below.

Product	Product Code
Aeroplane	01AE
Astronaut	
Alphabet Blocks	

(2 marks)

(c)   Identify whether the following statements regarding manual bookkeeping systems are true or false.

	True	False
The sales returns daybook is one of the books of prime entry		
A manual bookkeeping system can decrease the risk of errors when moving data from the books of prime entry to the ledgers		

(2 marks)

(d)   Identify whether the following statements regarding digital bookkeeping systems are true or false.

	True	False
A digital bookkeeping system automatically reconciles receivables and payables ledgers to the control accounts		
A digital bookkeeping system automatically balances the cash book		

(2 marks)

TASK 2 (10 MARKS)

This task is about principles of double-entry bookkeeping.

(a) **Identify the classification of each account.**

Account	Classification
Trade payable	
Computer equipment	
Discounts received	

Picklist: Asset, Liability, Income, Expense, Capital

(3 marks)

Kante Co has a total capital balance of £16,540 and total liabilities of £34,500.

(b) **Calculate the value of assets in Kante Co.**

£

(1 mark)

(c) **Identify the dual effect of each transaction by matching the dual effect from the picklist to the transaction identified. You should ignore VAT in this task.**

Transaction	Dual effect
A sale of goods on credit	
Received a new loan from the bank	
Payment to a credit supplier using the bank	
A purchase of a motor vehicle for cash	
Payment of fuel expenses for cash	
Receipt of cash from the owner	

Picklist
Increase in assets and capital
Increase in assets and income
Increase in expenses, decrease in assets
Increase in assets and liabilities
Both increase and decrease an asset
Decrease in assets and liabilities

(6 marks)

TASK 3 (10 MARKS)

This task is about processing customer invoices or credit notes and entering in daybooks.

A sales invoice is being prepared from the delivery note below.

Jeff's Jackets
Delivery note no. 4021

01 Dec 20X2

Customer account code: JJ01

500 cases of product A, product code 03FE

The list price of the goods was £40 per case plus VAT. Jeff's Jackets are to be given a 10% trade discount.

(a) Calculate the amounts to be included in the invoice.

	£
Amount before discount	
Discount given	
Amount after discount	
VAT	
Total	

(5 marks)

(b) Which daybook will the above transaction be entered in?

	£
Sales daybook	
Sales returns daybook	
Cash book	
Discounts allowed daybook	

(1 mark)

(c) Complete the daybook entry below.

Date 20X2	Customer code	Invoice No:	Total £	VAT £	Net £
1 Dec		142			

(4 marks)

TASK 4 (10 MARKS)

This task is about processing receipts from customers.

Kante Co has received a cheque for £223 for the settlement of two invoices below. In addition to the two invoices, Kante Co had also given Buckley Co a credit note for £25 for faulty goods it had previously supplied.

Kante Co	
Invoice number 193	
To: Buckley Co 19 October 20X2	
	£
10 units product XJ45 @ £12 each	120.00
VAT @ 20%	24.00
Total	144.00

Kante Co	
Invoice number 194	
To: Buckley Co 20 October 20X2	
	£
5 units product XJ44 @ £9 each	45.00
VAT @ 20%	9.00
Total	54.00

(a)   **Complete the following statement:**

Buckley Co has _____GAP 1_____ so _____GAP 2_____.

Gap 1	✓
Overpaid Kante Co	
Underpaid Kante Co	
Paid Kante Co the correct amount	

Gap 2	✓
A refund is due	
A request for further payment should be made	
No further action is required	

(2 marks)

Kante Co has also received a cheque for £483 for the settlement of two invoices below. The cheque was received on 1 December 20X2. Kante Co offers Moran Co a 5% prompt payment if the payment is made within 20 days of the invoice date.

Kante Co	
Invoice number 213	
To: Moran Co 22 October 20X2	
	£
20 units product XJ45 @ £12 each	240.00
VAT @ 20%	48.00
Total	288.00

Kante Co	
Invoice number 219	
To: Moran Co 23 October 20X2	
	£
20 units product XJ44 @ £9 each	180.00
VAT @ 20%	36.00
Total	216.00

(b)   Complete the following statement:

Moran Co has _____GAP 1_____ so _____GAP 2_____.

Gap 1	✓
Overpaid Kante Co	
Underpaid Kante Co	
Paid Kante Co the correct amount	

Gap 2	✓
A refund is due	
A request for further payment should be made	
No further action is required	

(2 marks)

Kante Co	
Invoice number 253	
To: Moran Co 25 November 20X2	
	£
20 units product XJ23 @ £30 each	600.00
VAT @ 20%	120.00
	————
Total	720.00

(c)   **If Moran Co pays the above invoice within 10 days and receives the prompt payment discount, what is the amount that Moran Co will pay?**

£

(1 mark)

(d)   **How would Kante Co categorise the discount taken by Moran Co?**

	✓
Income	
Expense	
Asset	
Liability	

(1 mark)

Kante Co issued the following invoice to Leighton Co:

Kante Co	
Invoice number 268	
To: Leighton Co 30 October 20X2	
	£
15 units product XJ45 @ £12 each	180.00
Bulk discount 10%	(18.00)
Net amount	162.00
VAT @ 20%	36.00
	————
Total	126.00

(e) **Which TWO errors have Kante Co made in the above invoice?**

	✓
The total product cost is incorrectly calculated	
The bulk discount should not be applied until Kante Co know if the payment will be made on time	
The VAT figure is incorrectly calculated	
The total invoice amount is incorrectly calculated	

(2 marks)

Kante Co received the following remittance advice from Croft Co.

Remittance advice 1 November 20X2	
Invoice	£
145	600.00
183	125.00
	———
Total	725.00

Kante Co' receivables ledger shows the following in respect of Croft:

Date 20X2	Details	Invoice number	Total £	VAT £	Net £
3 Oct	Croft Co	145	600	500	100
8 Oct	Croft Co	183	150	25	125

(f) **Identify if the invoices have been paid correctly or not**

	Paid correctly ✓	Not paid correctly ✓
Invoice 145		
Invoice 183		

(2 marks)

TASK 5 (10 MARKS)

This task is about processing supplier invoices or credit notes and entering in daybooks.

The following invoice has been received from the credit supplier Clanker Co for goods that were received on 10 December 20X2. The warehouse staff have confirmed that the goods were received correctly. Clanker Co has a supplier code which is CLA05.

Clanker Co, Invoice No. 1365	
To: Kante Co, 10 Dec 20X2	
60 units of product YT653 @ £46 each	£2,760.00
VAT	£552.00
Total	£3,312.00

(a)   **Enter the details into the missing sections in the daybook.**

Date 20X2	Supplier code	Invoice No:	Total £	VAT £	Net £
10 Dec		1365			

(4 marks)

(b)   **Which daybook would this be entered into?**

	✓
Supplier's daybook	
Purchases daybook	
Cash book	
Sales daybook	

(1 mark)

Kante Co discovered later that three of the units were damaged and contacted the supplier in order to receive a credit note. This was agreed by Clanker Co and the credit note was issued before the payment from Kante Co was due.

(c)   **Which TWO of these items represent the dual effect in Kante Co's records when the credit note is received?**

	✓
Liabilities will decrease	
Assets will increase	
Expenses will decrease	
Income will increase	

(2 marks)

The purchasing department in Kante Co have recently received another purchase invoice from Clanker Co. They have then compared it to the purchase order and have noted some discrepancies.

Purchase order PO682

To: Clanker Co, 18 Dec 20X2

Order details:

15 units of product YT653 @ £46 each

Terms: 30 days

Clanker Co

Invoice No. 1940

To: Kante Co
19 Dec 20X2

15 units of product YT653 @ £46 each	£690.00
VAT	£103.50
Total	£3,312.00

Payment will be due on 3 January 20X3

(d) Identify the THREE discrepancies between the purchase order and the purchase invoice.

	✓
Net amount	
VAT calculation	
Total amount	
Payment terms	
Product supplied	
Quantity supplied	
Unit price	

(3 marks)

TASK 6 (10 MARKS)

This task is about processing payments to suppliers.

The two invoices below were received on 3 January from credit suppliers of Kante Co who offer prompt payment discounts.

Invoices:

	Groves Ltd	
	Invoice number 6836	
To: Kante Co	3 January 20X3	
		£
250 product code H43 @ £4.80 each		1,200.00
VAT @ 20%		240.00
		————
Total		1,440.00
Terms: 5% prompt payment discount if payment is received within 10 days of the invoice date.		

	Moore Ltd	
	Invoice number 578	
To: Kante Co	3 January 20X3	
		£
140 product code TR6 @ £6.50 each		910.00
VAT @ 20%		182.00
		————
Total		1,092.00
Terms: 10% prompt payment discount if payment is received within 5 days of the invoice date.		

(a)   Calculate the amount to be paid to each supplier if the prompt payment discount is taken and when the payment needs to be made.

Supplier	£	Date by which to make the payment
Groves Ltd		
Moore Ltd		

(4 marks)

Kante Co has received a query from Bloomer Ltd, one of its suppliers. A member of the payments team sent Bloomer Ltd one cheque for £14,630 but did not send a remittance with it, so you have been asked to identify what amounts the cheques are paying off. Bloomer have sent a statement below.

Bloomer Ltd Customer statement		
To: Kante Co		
Date 20X2	**Details**	**Transaction amount £**
12 Dec	Invoice 345	10,450
13 Dec	Invoice 346	3,210
21 Dec	Invoice 347	2,000
21 Dec	Credit note 101	1,030
22 Dec	Invoice 348	230
27 Dec	Invoice 349	820
28 Dec	Credit note 102	50

(b)   Which FOUR items should now be removed from the Bloomer Ltd customer statement now that the payment has been made?

Details	✔
Invoice 345	
Invoice 346	
Invoice 347	
Credit note 101	
Invoice 348	
Invoice 349	

(4 marks)

(c)   What will be the amount remaining as owed to Bloomer Ltd?

£ [   ]

(1 mark)

(d) Which of the following statements regarding remittance advices is correct?

Details	✓
Remittances are sent to the inventory department to advise them inventory has been paid for	
Remittances are sent to the customer to advise them of the amount being paid	
Remittances are sent to the bank to confirm payment is to be made	
Remittances are sent to the supplier to advise them of the amount being paid	

(1 mark)

TASK 7 (8 MARKS)

This task is about processing transactions in the cash book.

One of the finance team went to the bank today and paid in two amounts, the details of which are as follows:

Receipts

Cheque 000642
From Broomes Co, paying all outstanding invoices
Total   £7,200 inclusive of VAT at 20%

Cash sales paid in
Total   £560

The cash sales all related to items that were zero-rated for VAT purposes.

Update the extract from the receipts section of the cash book below.

Details	General ledger code	Total £	VAT £	Net £
Broomes Co	Picklist			
Cash sales	Picklist			

General ledger code picklist: 3463 Trade Receivables, 7420 Trade Payables, 6200 Sales, 5600 Purchases

(8 marks)

TASK 8 (6 MARKS)

This task is about processing transactions in the petty cash book.

Kante Co maintains an analytical petty cash book. At the end of the month, one of the accounts team at Kante Co withdraw enough money from the bank to ensure the balance on petty cash is at £300.

Details of the transactions in the petty cash book for the last month are shown below.

Petty cash-book

Date 20X3	Details	Amount £	Date 20XX	Details	Amount £	VAT £	Office expenses £
			15 Jan	Team lunch	60.00	10.00	50.00
			17 Jan	Coffee and milk	15.00	2.50	12.50

(a)   **What will be the entries required at 31 January to restore the total of the petty cash back up to £300?**

Details	Amount £	Debit ✓	Credit ✓

Details picklist: Amount, Balance b/d, Balance c/d, Cash from bank

(3 marks)

(b)   **What is the entry made in the petty cash book to record the closing balance on 30 June?**

Details	Amount £	Debit ✓	Credit ✓

Details picklist: Amount, Balance b/d, Balance c/d, Cash from bank

(3 marks)

TASK 9 (6 MARKS)

This task is about processing recurring entries.

Today's date is 20 January 20X3. Your supervisor has asked you to set up a recurring payment for services for confidential waste disposal for a one-year fixed-term contract. The total amount is for £660 a year, payable in monthly instalments on the 28th day of each month.

(a) **Set up the recurring entry.**

Transaction type	Details	Start date	Frequency	End date	Amount £
Recurring payment					

Picklists:

Details	✓
640 – Bank	
7420 – Trade payables	
1560 – Office expenses	
5600 – Purchases	

Start date	✓
20/01/20X3	
28/01/20X3	
28/02/20X3	
28/12/20X3	

Frequency	✓
Weekly	
Monthly	
Quarterly	
Annually	

End date	✓
20/01/20X4	
28/01/20X4	
28/02/20X4	
28/12/20X3	

(5 marks)

(b) **Which ONE of the following is true regarding recurring entries in a computerised bookkeeping system?**

	✓
The system makes sure the entries will be in the correct codes	
There is no scope for human error	
Entries will be made that automatically balance	
Individuals will still have to manually balance the cash book	

(1 mark)

TASK 10 (10 MARKS)

This task is about transferring data from the books of prime entry.

Today's date is 31 January 20X3 and you are responsible for transferring entries from the daybooks to the general ledger.

The totals of the purchases daybook of Kante Co are shown below. Some of the entries for transferring the item to the general ledger below have been filled in.

Date 20X3	Details	Total £	VAT £	Net £
31 Jan	Totals	6,804.00	1,134.00	5,670.00

(a) **What will be the entries in the general ledger?**

Account name	Amount £	Debit ✓	Credit ✓
Purchases			
VAT	1,134		
Payables ledger control			

(5 marks)

The totals of the discounts received daybook of Kante Co are shown below. Some of the entries for transferring the item to the general ledger below have been filled in.

Date 20X3	Details	Total £	VAT £	Net £
31 Jan	Totals	408	68	340

(b) **What will be the entries in the general ledger?**

Account name	Amount £	Debit ✓	Credit ✓
Discounts received			
VAT	68		
Payables ledger control			

(5 marks)

TASK 11 (10 MARKS)

This task is about totalling and balancing ledger accounts.

The customer account below is ready to be totalled and balanced at 31 January 20X3.

Swain Ltd

Date 20X3	Details	Amount £	Date 20X3	Details	Amount £
3 Jan	Invoice 932	9,450	8 Jan	Payment	14,630
9 Jan	Invoice 984	6,430			
16 Jan	Invoice 993	4,240			

(a)   Identify the entry required to record the closing balance on 31 January 20X3.

Detail	Amount £	Debit ✓	Credit ✓

Detail picklist: Balance b/d, balance c/d

(3 marks)

(b)   Calculate the amount that will be entered in each debit and credit column after the closing balance has been recorded.

£

(1 mark)

(c)   On which side of the ledger account would each item be shown in a supplier's ledger account?

Details	Debit ✓	Credit ✓
Purchase		
Discount received		
Payment made		

(3 marks)

(d)   On which side would the opening balance be recorded for each of the following accounts?

Details	Debit ✓	Credit ✓
Land and buildings		
Capital		
Loan from bank		

(3 marks)

Section 4

MOCK ASSESSMENT ANSWERS

TASK 1 (10 MARKS)

This task is about manual and digital bookkeeping systems.

(a)   Which document or report would be used for each of the purposes below?

	Document or report
To identify which specific invoices are being paid off when sending payment	Remittance
To issue a refund, write off an amount owed following a return of goods	Credit note
To show the detail of the goods sold and total price	Sales invoice
To show details of the amounts owed from each customer	Receivables ledger

(4 marks)

(b)   Identify the correct product codes for the items below.

Product	Product Code
Aeroplane	01AE
Astronaut	03AS
Alphabet Blocks	02AL

(2 marks)

Feedback: The correct alphabetical order here is Aeroplane, Alphabet blocks, Astronaut

(c)   Identify whether the following statements regarding manual bookkeeping systems are true or false.

	True	False
The sales returns daybook is one of the books of prime entry	✓	
A manual bookkeeping system can decrease the risk of errors when moving data from the books of prime entry to the ledgers		✓

(2 marks)

Feedback: Human error is possible when transferring data from daybooks to the ledgers in a manual system

(d) **Identify whether the following statements regarding digital bookkeeping systems are true or false.**

	True	False
A digital bookkeeping system automatically reconciles receivables and payables ledgers to the control accounts	✓	
A digital bookkeeping system automatically balances the cash book	✓	

(2 marks)

TASK 2 (10 MARKS)

This task is about principles of double-entry bookkeeping.

(a) **Identify the classification of each account.**

Account	Classification
Trade payable	Liability
Computer equipment	Asset
Discounts received	Income

(3 marks)

(b) **Calculate the amount of assets in Kante Co.**

£51,040

(1 mark)

Feedback:

Assets – Liabilities = Capital

Therefore, Assets = Capital + liabilities = £16,540 + £34.500 = £51,040

(c) **Identify the dual effect of each transaction by matching the dual effect from the picklist to the transaction identified. You should ignore VAT in this task.**

Transaction	Dual effect
A sale of goods on credit	Increase in assets and income
Received a new loan from the bank	Increase in assets and liabilities
Payment to a credit supplier using the bank	Decrease in assets and liabilities
A purchase of a motor vehicle for cash	Both increase and decrease an asset
Payment of fuel expenses for cash	Increase in expenses, decrease in assets
Receipt of cash from the owner	Increase in assets and capital

(6 marks)

Feedback:

A sale of goods on credit: Dr Receivables, Cr Revenue. Received a new loan: Dr Cash, Cr Loan liability. Payment to a credit supplier: Dr Payables, Cr Cash. Purchase MV: Dr Non-current assets, Cr Cash. Payment for fuel: Dr Fuel expense, Cr Cash. Receipt of cash from the owner: Dr Cash, Cr Capital

TASK 3 (10 MARKS)

This task is about processing customer invoices or credit notes and entering in daybooks.

(a) **Calculate the amounts to be included in the invoice.**

	£
Amount before discount	20,000
Discount given	(2,000)
Amount after discount	18,000
VAT	3,600
Total	21,600

(5 marks)

(b) **Which daybook will the above transaction be entered in?**

	✓
Sales daybook	✓
Sales returns daybook	
Cash book	
Discounts allowed daybook	

(1 mark)

(c) **Complete the daybook entry below.**

Date 20X2	Customer code	Invoice No:	Total £	VAT £	Net £
1 Dec	JJ01	142	21,600	3,600	18,000

(4 marks)

TASK 4 (10 MARKS)

This task is about processing receipts from customers.

(a) **Complete the following statement:**

Buckley Co has _____GAP 1_____ so _____GAP 2_____.

Gap 1	✓
Overpaid Kante Co	✓
Underpaid Kante Co	
Paid Kante Co the correct amount	

Gap 2	✓
A refund is due	✓
A request for further payment should be made	
No further action is required	

(2 marks)

Feedback: Buckley Co should have paid Kante Co £173 (£144 + £54 – £25)

(b) **Complete the following statement:**

Moran Co has _____GAP 1_____ so _____GAP 2_____.

Gap 1	✓
Overpaid Kante Co	
Underpaid Kante Co	✓
Paid Kante Co the correct amount	

Gap 2	✓
A refund is due	
A request for further payment should be made	✓
No further action is required	

(2 marks)

Feedback: Moran Co should have paid Kante Co £504 (£288 + £216). As the invoices were paid after 20 days, no prompt payment discount is applicable

(c) **If Moran Co pays the above invoice within 10 days and receives the prompt payment discount, what is the amount that Moran Co will pay?**

£684.00

(1 mark)

Feedback: (£720 × 95%) = £684.00.

(d) **How would Kante Co categorise the discount taken by Moran Co?**

	✓
Income	
Expense	✓
Asset	
Liability	

(1 mark)

(e) **Which TWO errors have Kante Co made in the above invoice?**

	✓
The total product cost is incorrectly calculated	
The bulk discount should not be applied until Kante Co know if the payment will be made on time	
The VAT figure is incorrectly calculated	✓
The total invoice amount is incorrectly calculated	✓

(2 marks)

Feedback:

The VAT should be on the net amount = £162 × 20% = £32.40

The VAT has been subtracted in error, rather than added to the invoice total

(f)   Identify if the invoices have been paid correctly or not.

	Paid correctly	Not paid correctly
Invoice 145	✓	
Invoice 183		✓

(2 marks)

Feedback: The VAT on Invoice 183 has not been paid

TASK 5 (10 MARKS)

(a)   Enter the details into the missing sections in the daybook.

Date 20X2	Supplier code	Invoice No:	Total £	VAT £	Net £
10 Dec	CLA05	1365	3,312.00	552.00	2,760.00

(4 marks)

(b)   Which daybook would this be entered into?

	✓
Suppliers daybook	
Purchases daybook	✓
Cash book	
Sales daybook	

(1 mark)

(c)   Which TWO of these items represent the dual effect in Kante Co's records when the credit note is received?

	✓
Liabilities will decrease	✓
Assets will increase	
Expenses will decrease	✓
Income will increase	

(2 marks)

Feedback: Dr Payables, Cr Purchase expense

(d) Identify the THREE discrepancies between the purchase order and the purchase invoice.

	✓
Net amount	
VAT calculation	✓
Total amount	✓
Payment terms	✓
Product supplied	
Quantity supplied	
Unit price	

(3 marks)

Feedback: The PO has no VAT calculation and no total amount given. The invoice payment date is less than the 30 days on the purchase order

TASK 6 (10 MARKS)

This task is about processing payments to suppliers.

(a) Calculate the amount to be paid to each supplier if the prompt payment discount is taken and when the payment needs to be made.

Supplier	£	Date by which to make the payment
Groves Ltd	1,368.00	13 January
Moore Ltd	982.80	8 January

(4 marks)

Feedback:

Groves Ltd £1,440 × 95% = £1368.00. Moore Ltd £1,092 × 90% = £982.80

(b) Which FOUR items should now be removed from the Bloomer Ltd customer statement now that the payment has been made?

Details	✓
Invoice 345	✓
Invoice 346	✓
Invoice 347	✓
Credit note 101	✓
Invoice 348	
Invoice 349	
Credit note 102	

(4 marks)

Feedback: £10,450 + £3,210 + £2,000 − £1,030 = £14,630

(c) **What will be the amount remaining as owed to Bloomer Ltd?**

£1,000

(1 mark)

Feedback: £230 + £820 – £50 = £1,000

(d) **Which of the following statements regarding remittance advices is correct?**

Details	✓
Remittance advices will be sent to the inventory department to advise them inventory has been paid for	
Remittance advices will be sent to the customer to advise them of the amount being paid	
Remittance advices will be sent to the bank to confirm payment is to be made	
Remittance advices will be sent to the supplier to advise them of the amount being paid	✓

(1 mark)

TASK 7 (8 MARKS)

Update the extract from the receipts section of the cash book below.

Details	General ledger code	Total £	VAT £	Net £
Broomes Co	3463 Trade Receivables	7,200	0	7,200
Cash sales	6200 Sales	560	0	560

(8 marks)

TASK 8 (6 MARKS)

(a) **What will be the entries required at 31 January to restore the total of the petty cash back up to £300?**

Details	Amount £	Debit ✓	Credit ✓
Cash from bank	75.00	✓	

(3 marks)

Feedback: £60 + £15 = £75 paid into petty cash

(b) **What is the entry made in the petty cash book to record the closing balance on 31 January?**

Details	Amount £	Debit ✓	Credit ✓
Balance c/d	300.00		✓

(3 marks)

Feedback: £300 will be in petty cash. As an asset it will be b/d on the debit side on 1 July and hence is c/d on the credit side at 30 June

TASK 9 (6 MARKS)

(a) **Set up the recurring entry**

Transaction type	Details	Start date	Frequency	End date	Amount £
Recurring payment	1560 – Office expenses	28/01/20X3	Monthly	28/12/20X3	55.00

(5 marks)

Feedback: The monthly payment is £660/12 = £55

(b) **Which ONE of the following is true regarding recurring entries in a computerised bookkeeping system?**

	✓
The system makes sure the entries will be in the correct codes	
There is no scope for human error	
Entries will be made that automatically balance	✓
Individuals will still have to manually balance the cash book	

(1 mark)

TASK 10 (10 MARKS)

(a) **What will be the entries in the general ledger?**

Account name	Amount £	Debit ✓	Credit ✓
Purchases	5,670	✓	
VAT	1,134	✓	
Payables ledger control	6,804		✓

(5 marks)

(b)   **What will be the entries in the general ledger?**

Account name	Amount £	Debit ✓	Credit ✓
Discounts received	340		✓
VAT	68		✓
Payables ledger control	408	✓	

(5 marks)

Feedback: A discount received reduces the amount of input VAT we can reclaim from HMRC and hence is a credit to the VAT control account

TASK 11 (10 MARKS)

(a)   **Identify the entry required to record the closing balance on 31 January 20X3.**

Detail	Amount £	Debit ✓	Credit ✓
Balance c/d	5,490		✓

(3 marks)

Feedback:

Swain Ltd

Date 20X3	Details	Amount £	Date 20X3	Details	Amount £
3 Jan	Invoice 932	9,450	8 Jan	Payment	14,630
9 Jan	Invoice 984	6,430			
16 Jan	Invoice 993	4,240		Balance c/d	5,490
		20,120			20,120
	Balance b/d	5,490			

(b)   **Calculate the amount that will be entered in each debit and credit column after the closing balance has been recorded.**

£20,120

(1 mark)

(c)   On which side of the ledger account would each item be shown in a supplier's ledger account?

Details	Debit ✓	Credit ✓
Credit purchase		✓
Discount received	✓	
Payment made	✓	

(3 marks)

(d)   On which side would the opening balance be recorded for each of the following accounts?

Details	Debit ✓	Credit ✓
Land and buildings	✓	
Capital		✓
Loan from bank		✓

(3 marks)